This Is No Ordinary Joy

SARAH SYMONS

FOR JOHN, MAYA AND LUKE

FOR ANJALI

AND FOR ALL THE SURVIVORS WHOSE COURAGE HAS
MADE THIS WORK POSSIBLE

Contents

PROLOGUE

Sitting on a cement floor in Calcutta, India, the soles of my bare feet black with grime. I'm wondering if you can get HIV infection through cracks in your heels. Later I found out you actually can so...*note to self: bring flip flops.* I've slept a total of six hours in the last three days. I'm dehydrated and hungry, having consumed nothing but bizarrely spicy potato chips and sugary tea since breakfast. I really need to go to the bathroom, but the one downstairs is sketchy, to say the least, so I'm holding out as long as possible.

This is the best day of my life.

I am surrounded by children, on my lap, filling in all the space around me. Their radiant faces show no sign of the circumstances that brought us all here. Some of their mothers are here with us too, in their bright saris, eyes so much older than their bodies. Most of these women are in their twenties or thirties, younger than me, but have seen and experienced unimaginable things for years, for decades. They are painfully thin and missing teeth. They move quietly, stoically, wearily through life. These mothers are heroes to me, because they show up here for their kids, because they find the strength to keep going at all.

These are the women and children of a Calcutta red light district. Here in Kidderpore, the oldest and poorest of the city's five red light areas, thousands of women and children live in conditions of extreme poverty and constant menace.

What am I doing here? Ten years ago I was a songwriter living on Cape Cod, running a small business writing and recording songs for soap operas. That was a long way from here, in every possible respect. My husband was an investment banker and we had a comfortable, prosperous life, with two small children.

Today, our lives are unrecognizable. Together, we run an agency working on some of the world's most desperate problems – human trafficking and slavery, child labor and child marriage, all manner of violence against women and girls. We work with some of the most deserving and courageous people on planet earth. They are survivors of slavery, kids born into brothels, children who once slept on scraps of cardboard in the streets. They are victims of gang rape and family torture and child marriage in societies which struggle to acknowledge these crimes, or to offer sufficient help to the victims of such crimes.

Working with these incredible women and girls has transformed my life and family, and has made me rich beyond my wildest dreams – rich in love and positive energy, that is.

Since I didn't know at first how to address the problems I witnessed, I had a sharp learning curve. I'm neither a saint, nor a superwoman. I'm a regular, opinionated, slightly frazzled woman trying to make a difference in a complex global problem. It's a continuing challenge, but by jumping in head first and casting my lot with women and children such as those in the red light area, I have found a life more joyful and insanely adventurous than I could ever have imagined.

My story is a series of miracles, some astonishing and life-changing, most small but nonetheless profound. The changes in my life sparked change in the lives of my family and friends, and ultimately in the lives of survivors and vulnerable girls on the other side of the world. When I truly opened my heart and life to their suffering, and began working to make their lives better, I found that help was everywhere. That was the most recurrent miracle.

This is my story and the story of the heroes I have met along the way, including many survivors who, despite having endured appalling suffering, still manage to manifest the most extraordinary joy. I have been guided by their courage, and by the miraculous power of love in this hurting world.

Along the way, in order to do this work, my husband and I sold our big house on Cape Cod and spent our life savings, plunging our family into financial uncertainty and stress. John gave up his job as an investment banker, and the salary, identity, and perks that went with it.

We witnessed many unmet needs in the field, so, working with local partners, we piloted a model which we have been perfecting over the last thirteen years through trial and error, discussion, mistakes and plenty of intense disagreement. At times I have reached (and still sometimes reach) the absolute limits of my ability to cope - with the pain of the survivor's lives, with the disappointments and frustrations and unexpected drama that come with running an international charity, and with the pressure of many futures depending on me.

This is the warts-and-all version of my story, holding back none of my mistakes, failures, doubts, marital conflict, every other kind of conflict, crisis, embarrassment, fear and loss.

I do this work as one member of a devoted team. I do it imperfectly. I do it with chronic worry and occasionally, gut-clenching fear. Most of all, I do it buoyed by and filled up by enormous love.

So let me tell you what really happened…

1 HAVE YOU EVER HAD CANCER BEFORE

September, 2001.   'Have you ever had cancer before?' the doctor asked my mother.

Cancer? Before?

This conversation made no sense. All the air was sucked out of the room. I rushed out into the hallway to begin breathing again. I suppose I should have stayed with my mother and stroked her hand or something, as she dealt with the news that her life as she knew it was over (in fact, her life was over, period, but thankfully the plain-spoken doctor drew the line at suggesting that).

I slunk back into the hospital room as soon as I could collect myself. My relentlessly positive attitude kicked back into gear. I was confident there would be treatments.

Three months later my mother was dead. She was 60 years old.

I never saw this coming and it ripped my world apart. The week before, my mother had been jogging three miles a day and helping me care for my baby and toddler. She had moved from England to Cape Cod, Massachusetts, to help me when I got pregnant with my daughter Maya. She uprooted her life to be near us, so I wouldn't feel isolated raising small children, as she had herself once felt.

My mother was one of the brightest lights in my life. She was an intensely committed mother and grandmother. She was a healthy woman with tremendous vitality.   Her name was Freedom, and I'm not being poetic. That really was her name. She changed it from Marion to Freedom on her fiftieth birthday.

Freedom did everything to support me and my family, helping John and I to raise our kids for three wonderful years. She loved and nurtured me for thirty-seven years, and every day as her daughter was a gift. When I came home from the hospital with baby Maya, exhausted, anemic and totally overwhelmed, Freedom came over every morning for a month at 6:00 am to watch the baby so I could sleep. She made soft-boiled eggs with toast fingers for dipping. She rocked the baby on her chest for three-hour naps. My friends who were also new mothers were bitterly envious, and who could blame them? Most new parents have to go it alone, and let's be honest, it's no picnic.

Then one day in September, 2001, my mom turned kind of yellow and began feeling nauseous. I was sure it was nothing to worry about, because I used to be that person, a happy-go-lucky kind of person who always expected the best and generally got it. That was why that day at the hospital found me hanging out in my mom's hospital room, chatting merrily, when the doctor came in to talk to us. I wasn't worried, because I expected it would be something minor.

The next three months brought bad news upon bad news, a failed operation to remove the tumor in Freedom's liver, and the gradual erosion of hope. I ceased to be happy-go-lucky. The nurses and doctors kindly but firmly dispossessed me of any false expectations that things might work out. The prognosis, they told us, was poor. Translation: '*You are going to die, and soon*'.

"I just don't get it… Why is it taking so long for my mom's stomach to start working again?" I asked a nurse after my mother had been on a feeding tube for six weeks.

"Well," she said carefully, glancing at the chart, "the prognosis *is* poor… Maybe her system is not healing because the cancer is progressing?" I bit my lip, turned away, and went home angry. "What a mean, negative nurse," I fumed later to John. "What is the point of saying something so grim?!"

Later, I understood. The nurse was trying to help me come to terms with reality. But in almost every book and movie, the heroine *recovers* from her cancer, and goes on to share her inspiring story with the world. I couldn't begin to accept that this would not happen for us.

A few weeks after the diagnosis, Freedom was given the option of an operation which had a thirty percent chance of buying her a few more years. She was ambivalent, but I begged her to try it. The morning of the operation, I woke up early and drove her to the hospital. She was naturally anxious, and rightly so, as it turned out. First the nurses could not find a vein and it took half an hour before they could start the anesthesia. It was an inauspicious start, and things went downhill from there. Six hours later, the doctor came to tell me the bad news. The operation had not been successful. I lost my composure and went into a kind of shock. I don't remember much about the next few days.

I do remember lurching through the hospital desperately seeking a chaplain or social worker during the operation. The rawness of my pain made people slightly uncomfortable, but I was too far gone to worry about that. A chaplain was sent to talk to me in the super-cozy waiting room they reserve for the truly pitiable, those whose loved ones' prognosis is poor. I told the chaplain I was hoping for a miracle, but that the odds were not in our favor.

"Hmmm," she said thoughtfully, "maybe you already had your miracle? Maybe your miracle is not what you think. Or maybe your miracle is still to come". When I was little, my mother suffered from life-threatening ulcerative colitis. After years of failed treatments, she went on a special diet and was instantly cured after suffering with the disease for fifteen years. Her doctors could not explain it. *Could this be the miracle the chaplain suggested?* I wasn't sure.

After the operation failed, the light went out of my life for a while. Caring for a baby and toddler, while juggling daily hospital visits through my own mounting despair, was truly awful. Impossible. Thank God for John, who somehow managed to patch me together each morning and night, and to fill in the gaps with the kids, winsome but demanding three-year-old Maya and easygoing one-year old Luke, just beginning to stagger on his tiny legs.

The hospital was hot and stuffy and smelled like a hospital. One evening, my mother asked me to buy her a fan. It was about 9:00 and I drove to Home Depot, which is open late, and bought her a fan. It was a rare moment of peace because I felt I could finally do something concrete to ease my mother's suffering. Unfortunately, the nurses wouldn't let us set up the fan because it wasn't sterile. This relatively minor setback was one of my darkest moments in the whole ordeal. It seemed there was nothing I could do to relieve my mother's pain and anxiety, and I felt completely helpless. My heart sunk back to its customary depths.

One night, Freedom asked me to pray aloud. "I can't pray," she confessed. "I haven't been able to pray since the operation". My mother was normally so wise, so strong and spiritually sound. Her illness brought on a deep depression that caused her to lose hope. Briefly I wondered if I was going to survive this experience.

Ten weeks after the operation, the hospital discharged Freedom to a nursing home, where at long last we were able to see an oncologist about the possibility of chemotherapy to buy her some time. The oncologist looked at my mother's x-rays and took blood tests, and then, as kindly as possible, he told us there was nothing whatsoever he could do. The cancer had advanced too quickly and the recovery from the operation had taken too long. My mother's liver was failing and she had only a few weeks left to live.

I had believed up until that moment that I had already given up hope, but the gut-punch I felt upon hearing those words proved that I was sadly mistaken. Apparently there was some tiny, ultra-resilient pocket of hope left in both me and my mother, because when the oncologist broke that final bad news, a shock wave plowed through the room and knocked us flat.

After the doctor left the room, tears began to fall silently down Freedom's face. I sat down on her bed, and stroked her head, but only for about one minute, because then I had to leave her there, alone. A friend was watching my kids and he had to go to work. I wish I had left my friend to deal with that relatively minor problem and stayed by my mother's side to share that last, crushing disappointment. In that morass of emotion and loss, it was hard to make rational decisions.

By the time we finally got Freedom home to our house a few days later, there was little time left. In movies, and I hope sometimes in real life, dying people get to come home and enjoy one last holiday or long weekend. Everybody laughs and cries and tells sweet stories from the past, the dying person gives sage advice, and everyone eats ice cream and finally comes to a place of peace.

For us, it wasn't like that at all. Freedom did not want anyone around except me and my brother, our children, and her sister. She was anxious about the prospect of losing control of her body. We signed up for hospice care which helped a lot.

Christmas was a somber occasion. That was when the hospice doctor prescribed morphine for Freedom's increasing pain. My mother became calm and at last comfortable. Giving her morphine injections right in the stomach took a little getting used to, but it was worth it. I stayed by her bedside most of the time, and didn't leave the house for five days.

On December 28th, I went out for a few hours to meet a friend for a drink. We were having fun, and at one point, I laughed out loud, for the first time in three months. At that exact moment, John called to tell me my mother had just died. She must have waited until the one time I went out, because it was too hard for her to leave me otherwise. I believe she sensed that I was laughing, that I would somehow be okay, and chose that moment to slip away.

2 A VERY BAD DAY

There was some relief when Freedom's suffering ended. However, her death left me grief-stricken, dealing with the worst loss of my life without the very person I turned to when things got rough.

Walking through an underground parking lot with my kids, I heard a cheery older woman's voice exclaim, "Look at your beautiful Mama!" My heart leapt, and for an instant the dull pain evaporated. That is exactly what Freedom used to say, in exactly that tone of voice. But of course, I immediately realized, that was another mama, another adoring grandmother. Freedom was gone and would not be coming back.

I have the bizarre need for people to think I have it together at all times. This added another level of strain, as I so obviously did not have it together but was compelled to try to make it seem like I did. *It's okay, I'm not really here*, I sometimes pretended to cheer myself up. Every morning, as soon as I woke up, I prayed for ten minutes for the strength to get out of bed and get through the day. I began setting an alarm so I would have ample time to lose it and pull it together again before the kids woke up.

On Freedom's birthday, May 5th, rain was falling in relentless sheets. It was gloomy, dark and cold, a typical New England spring day. It was a suitably somber setting for a day I'd been so anxiously anticipating. I was learning that when you lose a loved one, these once special days become the most dreaded.

Wisely, I had hired a babysitter for Maya and Luke, as I knew I would be fit company for neither man nor beast. I spent the morning driving around Cape Cod in the pouring rain, pulling over to sob in various parking lots when my emotions became overwhelming. Eventually, I found myself in the Kmart parking lot, head on the steering wheel, blubbering away, truly a pitiable sight.

Ever since losing Freedom, I had been in the habit of talking with her, at various moments throughout each day, asking for her help and insights in running my life. I also kept up a running commentary with God. These silent monologues were my greatest comfort. On Freedom's birthday, I was too despairing to talk to either one of them. I wasn't exactly angry at God. I just felt, on that day, disgruntled and alone. And if you can't say something nice, don't say anything at all, that's my policy.

However, I really do love chatting to dead people, so I decided to reach out to another lost loved one. Phillip was a teenage boy that John and I had mentored in a program for homeless kids in Harlem several years earlier. He was six years old when I first met him, a tiny, brown-skinned, red-headed boy dragging a heavy wooden panel through an abandoned lot we had fashioned into a park, helping us set up an arts workshop for the other children.

Phillip was sixteen years old when he was murdered, trying to keep violent gangs out of his Brooklyn neighborhood. He always put himself on the line to protect his family and friends, but we all hoped this trait would lead him to a career in law enforcement, not to an early death. The death of a child is always tragic, and I had been devastated by Phillip's death, but a few years had passed since that loss. The wound was scarred over, and I could now cope with talking to Phillip, a boy who knew much about loss, even before he died.

So I reached out to my young friend, asking him to put in a word for me - with God, with my mother, with anyone out there listening. I don't believe in praying for signs, and I resisted the temptation to do so. I was just hoping for some sense that my prayers were being heard. "Phillip, you have to help me out here," I said out loud. "I don't how to do this. Could you put in a word for me up there? Can somebody up there help a woman out!?"

I knew I was being dramatic, but no one was there to see it, and talking to Phillip made me feel much better. It always helps to share your troubles, even if the person you share them with is dead. After my heart-to-heart with Phillip, I was able to face the rest of the day in a happier frame of mind. I was incredibly grateful for that, and it would have been enough.

It turned out there was more good news to come. When I got home that evening, there was a message from my friend Tracy with some wonderful news. Tracy is a music agent, and she had just succeeded in getting one of my songs placed in a feature film. This was a breakthrough because it was my first song placement in a film. My songs had until then only been placed in television, primarily in soap operas (love and death scenes were my specialty).

I was deeply comforted by this experience. I felt as if God had heard my cry for help, and provided something really special to counteract my despair. I imagined my mother close at hand, pulling strings on my behalf.

The film starred Emmy Rossum, who was to sing my composition over the opening titles. It was a wonderful opportunity, and I was ecstatic, jumping for joy by the end of the voicemail. Then Tracy told me the name of the song that had been chosen. It was 'Street of Dreams - a Song for Phillip'. This was a song I had written about Phillip shortly after he died. The title refers to Calle de Suenos (Street of Dreams) the art park in East Harlem where I had first met Phillip as a little boy.

I know a place, where fear cannot find you,

I know a place where sorrow and pain they cannot follow you.

Ever since I've known you, you've been searching, for the right in wrong, for the truth in life.

Ever since I've known you, you've been reaching for something that is just out of sight...

Will you meet me there, up at the Street of Dreams? Will you meet me there someday? Someday...

This surreal experience helped me turn a corner in my grief. I soon found myself able to get up each morning without praying for 10 minutes for the the strength to face the day. Gradually, there were more and more moments of serenity, good feelings, even spontaneous joy. Maybe this was the miracle the hospital chaplain had suggested might yet come my way? Or perhaps it was my mother blowing out her metaphoric birthday candles and wishing me this good fortune. Or maybe, dare I say it, this was the sign for which I had refused to ask.

3 THE DAY MY GOD DIED

March, 2003: I couldn't believe I was watching a movie star perform my song on a giant screen. I may have even shrieked, ever so softly. Nine months had passed since my 'Sixth Sense' moment with Phillip. I was sitting in a fancy-pants theater at the Tribeca Film Festival, watching Emmy Rossum perform my song over the opening credits of the film 'Nola'. This was the moment I'd been hoping and working for over the previous three years. I felt sure this was the beginning of a new phase of my life. This breakthrough was sure to take my musical career to a whole new level.

The day after the premiere, still all aglow, I attended a panel discussion in the morning. In the afternoon, I had just a few hours before our film release party in the evening. Since I had a free pass to see any film at Tribeca, I looked over the film listings with great expectations. I love movies and the long list felt a little like Christmas - so many presents to open, which one to open first?!

But alas, this particular festival was shaping up to be a pretty sparse Christmas for me. I only had a three-hour window in which to see films, and not one of my top choices was screening during that time frame. My second or third choices were likewise unavailable. In fact, the only film I could find was 'The Day My God Died,' a documentary about human trafficking of young girls between Nepal and India. Because I now run a human rights charity, you might think I would be the sort of earnest, socially conscious person who would react with great excitement to a film like that.

To be completely honest, I was not excited at all. Instead, I was resistant and slightly fearful. Full disclosure: I had absolutely no intention of going to that movie. I may have physically recoiled - just a little - from that grim title in the film catalog. 'Well, I won't be going to that one,' I said to myself.

It's too upsetting.

I'm here to celebrate.

It's the wrong time in my life. I've got two little kids.

I've been through a year of grief and it will be too harsh for me right now.

Anyway, what's the point? I won't be able to do anything about it.

All that being said, I could hardly attend the Tribeca Film Festival and not see a single film other than the one in which my song was featured. That would be pathetic. That would feel like a missed opportunity. I had a free pass to this festival and by golly I wasn't going to waste it. I scoured the list again.

Same problem. There truly was no other option. It was 'The Day My God Died' or nothing. Finally, I decided to face down my fears and give it a shot. Perhaps I would learn something, or become a better person, I told myself, rallying to the occasion.

'The Day My God Died' changed my life that afternoon. It was ninety minutes of unbelievable suffering and abuse, loss and despair, courage and relentless hope. Normally, I don't cry much (did I mention I'm British?). I had cried very little even in my deepest grief, and certainly not in public. But during that film screening, tears flowed down my face for ninety minutes straight. I was literally dehydrated from all that crying. I had understood vaguely that there was slavery in the world. I had thought it was a relatively rare occurrence, tragic but rare, an individual crime affecting small groups of unfortunate individuals.

I had no idea there were millions of slaves in the world (40 million as of the 2017 UN report). I couldn't believe that many of them are children and teens, that people are enslaved in every country of the world, for sexual exploitation, for domestic service, on farms, in factories, in quarries, making steel, making bricks, and worse. I was devastated by the fact that the average age of entry into brothel slavery is in the early teens.

The film profiled several Nepali girls who had been trafficked into brothels in India, one at age twelve, one at age seven, one at nineteen, trafficked with her baby daughter. The twelve-year-old was raped by six men for three days to 'break her in'. She contracted AIDS during her years in the brothel. She is the one who gave the film its title, describing the day she was trafficked as 'the day my god died'.

No, this can't be real.

The seven-year-old suffered a spinal injury from the weight of adult men on her small body. She will always have a limp and back pain. She spent much of her childhood chained under a bed.

This can't be happening to millions of women and girls every day.

The hardest part, many of the girls said, was that they could cry and scream for help but no one would ever come. People on the streets looked at them with disgust. Even if they were rescued, their families often would not take them back. Everything was lost. Everything was ruin.

I found it impossible to accept that slavery was occurring at this magnitude and that most of the world was oblivious to it. Shouldn't we be marching in the streets, dropping everything, rushing in to the brothels and factories and mines to rescue these women and children, and men? There should be a deafening international public outcry, an uproar which could not be ignored. Instead, for the most part, there was silence – silence and inaction.

How did I not know about this? Was I simply naive and not paying attention? I didn't think so. I considered myself fairly aware of current events and world issues. Nonetheless, I had just learned I had an unacceptable level of ignorance about what some of my sisters and brothers around the world were enduring. I've since learned that like me, many people are afraid to look at the issue of slavery at all, not wanting to be pulled down into that darkness, afraid that they will not be able to do anything.

Luckily for me, 'The Day My God Died' was not just a shocking exposé. It was a call to action. Beyond all that inhumanity and pain, there was something even more powerful. There was hope. There was courage and selflessness. Survivors in the film, who had been sold into brothels as children, had created an Underground Railroad to rescue others and to prevent them from being trafficked in the first place. The girls went back into the brothels from which they were rescued, alongside rescue agencies and police. They used their unique knowledge of the brothels to pull other girls to freedom. They knew to look under the floorboards, behind the walls, in rolled-up carpets. The trauma and fear they faced must have been monumental, going back to the places where they were hurt and humiliated, tortured and treated as less than human.

Survivors in the film were going door to door and village to village in the remotest areas, handing out flyers with cartoons depicting trafficking for illiterate people, and telling their stories in an effort to prevent other girls from being tricked or sold. In societies such as Nepal, where so much stigma is attached to prostitution, it is an act of heroism for a survivor to share her story with strangers. Their actions were revolutionary.

I knew two things for sure after seeing that film. I knew I *had* to find a way to help these girls, and I knew my own life would never be the same.

The film forced me to radically rethink my life and values. It shook me out of my ignorance and inaction into the greatest adventure of my life. Earlier that day, as I had obsessively checked and rechecked the listings for a more appealing film, I had been unwilling and afraid to witness the suffering of trafficked girls, let alone try to help them. Before the final credits rolled, I knew I was on a whole new path.

By the time I saw that film, I had been feeling for a while that my life wasn't fitting quite right. I often wondered whether writing songs for soap operas was really what I was put on this earth to do. My mother's premature death had given me a greater appreciation of the shortness and preciousness of life.

Before I could figure out what I was supposed to be doing with my life, I first had to open my eyes to the entire world around me, including the ugliest parts. It hurts to witness such suffering, but it was a necessary step to finding the place where my greatest passion met the world's greatest need. When I found the place where I was needed most – the world of extreme gender violence - I was seized by an irresistible urge to take action.

"So… I've seen a film that is going to change my life, I told John over coffee a few hours after seeing the film. I might have added, 'and yours too, and the kids lives, and the lives of a bunch of other people we don't even know yet', but of course I had no way of knowing any of that.

To John's credit, he looked neither surprised nor skeptical. He barely raised an eyebrow. "Cool," he said, with a small nod, and reached for another bite of salad.

I told him about the girls in 'The Day My God Died'. I shared my conviction that if these young girls, after all they had endured, could put their lives on the line to rescue others, then there must be *something* I could do to help them.

But where to start? I knew so little about the issue. I had only just learned it existed. I lived in Cape Cod, Massachusetts, not in India or Nepal where the documentary was focused. I wasn't likely to be able to conduct brothel rescues or investigations. I wasn't a millionaire or an investigative journalist. I had two small children at home. It wasn't easy to figure out where to start.

A few days after the film festival, I emailed the two agencies profiled in the film. These were Maiti Nepal in Kathmandu and Sanlaap in Calcutta. I wrote that I had learned of their work through the film and was committed to helping in any way, from fundraising to knitting baby clothes. I don't actually know how to knit, but I figured I could learn anything if it would help. Perhaps things would have been easier if they had taken me up on the knitwear…

I now know that agencies like these receive heaps of letters from earnest wannabe volunteers, people who have been compelled to action by a documentary or book. In most cases the people already doing the work are much too busy to respond to every vague offer of help. Thus, I was extremely lucky that someone at Maiti Nepal got right back to me. She told me that Maiti Nepal had two volunteers already working for them in the U.S. and suggested that I might be able to work with them.

'Do you live anywhere near Boston?' she inquired. Out of the vast geography of the United States, Maiti Nepal's U.S. headquarters was just one hour from my house on Cape Cod! This was one of many small signs along the way that made me feel I was on the right path.

The people at Maiti Nepal introduced me to Joe and Brigitte Cazalis-Collins, who represented Maiti Nepal in the United States. I begged Joe and Brigitte to let me help in any way. Thankfully they agreed, and I spent the next year volunteering with their organization. I drove up to Boston a few times a month to help with fundraising and messaging.

By day, I was taking care of the kids, then in preschool, and writing songs for television, though my passion for that career path was waning. Up until that year, I had pursued my musical career with a single-minded passion. Now it was drifting to the back burner. Instead I felt driven to protect the world's forgotten girls, to take responsibility for some of them as I did for my own children. My mothering instincts were expanding to encompass the world. In comparison to that, my earlier ambitions seemed less compelling.

By night, I studied up on trafficking and gender violence online, and read every book I could find on the subject. I was itching to do more, but Maya and Luke were still tiny, and caring for them was a full-time job. I also had much yet to learn. Still, I was aching for a deeper involvement.

After I had been working with Joe and Brigitte for a year, they invited me to join them on an upcoming visit to Nepal, to see the Maiti Nepal shelter for myself and to meet the survivors there.

"I'd love to, but I just can't…" I started to say. Before I finished my sentence, I realized it just might be possible. I went home and discussed the idea with John, who was very supportive of my going. My aunt offered to help take care of the kids while I was away. I realized there was nothing in the world I wanted more than to go to that shelter in Nepal. That very night I booked my flight.

There, it was done. Too late to change my mind.

4 THE JOURNEY OF A THOUSAND MILES BEGINS...

Journal entry, Kathmandu, Nepal: *'Looking into that mother's eyes, I witnessed the utter absence of hope… the one thing we humans cannot seem to live without. She clutched a dog-eared Polaroid of her teenage daughter who had disappeared eleven days earlier, and who she feared had been trafficked to India.*

The look on that woman's face is burned into my memory. I could only imagine the unbearable agony I would feel if my child was missing and presumed to be trafficked into a brothel. She must have known she might never see her daughter again, but she had traveled three days on foot to post her crumpled Polaroid on the shelter's long wall of missing daughters. It was the only chance she had. This was by far the worst suffering I had ever witnessed'

For the four years prior to my first trip to Asia, I had been caring for two babies, then toddlers, then small children, and briefly for my mother as she died in my home. Like most mothers, I had moments (weeks, months!) of identity crisis, feeling drained, bored, lonely, overwhelmed by the endless needs of others. When my children were babies, I started each day with great enthusiasm, but by 11:00 a.m. I just wanted to say, 'Thanks, you've been a great audience,' and leave the building. Alas, at that point there would still be at least eight hours to go.

So, to be honest, the first thing I felt as I got on that airplane to Nepal (via Newark, via London, via Qatar, which in case you ever need to know, is actually pronounced 'Cutter') was freedom and exhilaration. Finally, after four years, I would have some time for myself! For eleven days, I would have the luxury of waking up in a hotel room, free of tiny plastic toys and sticky Cheerios and dog hair and socks that mysteriously I was the only one who could ever find. I would awake alone, eat my breakfast in serenity, do a few yoga stretches (these never actually materialized) and not have to cook or clean a thing. I was excited about the possibility that I could contribute something to the world, beyond taking care of babies and writing songs for soap operas.

Flying by myself seemed easy, compared to the past few trips with mewling, puking infants, thirty plus hours of travel notwithstanding. Briefly in Qatar, I had a minor hallucinogenic experience brought on by sheer exhaustion, but a hearty English breakfast of egg and chips soon restored me to wholeness.

After so many hours of travel, I was a wreck when I landed in Kathmandu. Somewhere in that endless journey, I had picked up a nagging cough which proved impervious to treatment. For the entire trip, I was to be racked with uncontrollable coughing, roughly thirty seconds out of every two minutes. Even the cough syrup I bought in Nepal, to which they thoughtfully added a small amount of morphine, brought me no relief.

It was embarrassing, because I was trying to blend in and not make a scene, and I knew many of the girls at Maiti Nepal had HIV/AIDS or tuberculosis, so my constant coughing felt doubly inappropriate. I was terrified of infecting someone, or even of seeming contagious. I washed my hands obsessively and ran outside for a private cough whenever possible. It felt like an undignified beginning to my new career fighting slavery.

Joe Collins met me at the airport with a warm smile and hug. I have never, before or since, been so happy to see another person's face at an airport. Joe suggested we go straight to Maiti Nepal, where he had a short meeting scheduled. I could meet the team and take a brief tour of the facility. It would only take an hour or so, he promised. Then I could go to the hotel to shower and rest.

I did not know then what I know now: visiting people in Asia is never brief. There are long greetings. There are long, easy silences. There are salty refreshments, and many cups of spicy chai with heaps of sugar. There are unhurried, thoughtful conversations, and then, with the end finally in view, there are drawn-out goodbyes.

Despite my fatigue, the shelter amazed me, even after seeing pictures and hearing about it for a whole year. It was a large brick complex of six buildings surrounding an open courtyard. The place was pulsing with life, babies, children, teens and young adults, survivors and their children.

Many girls are pregnant or have a baby when they are rescued from the brothels. Traffickers make sure the girls have a child in the first year or two, because once the girls are mothers, chains and bars are no longer needed to keep them captive. Their own children make the perfect chains, because a mother will never leave her child behind. The brothel-keepers keep the babies under strict control and some girls are not allowed to see their children for months at a time. This is another means of psychological control and abuse.

The young mothers at Maiti Nepal had been rescued along with their children, or had given birth after rescue. The babies stayed with their mothers in the dorm rooms, four to six beds to a room, simple, clean and comfortable. Bright, hand-dyed textiles covered the beds. Photos of the girls, their children, Bollywood stars and religious icons covered the walls.

Wherever we walked in the shelter complex, children would smile and wave, clasping their tiny hands in a 'Namaste' greeting. Despite the fog of jet-lag, I felt completely at home. I wished I could stay longer and get to know everyone there. These girls had seen the worst that life can offer and still they managed to smile, to get on with life, to take my hand and proudly show me around their home. In such circumstances, all pretenses and foolish worries become meaningless. Everything came into perspective.

Four *hours* later, bleary-eyed, I finally stumbled into my hotel room and fell into a dreamless slumber. I had been awake for the better part of fifty hours, the longest I had ever gone without sleep.

The next morning at dawn, we returned to the shelter and lined up with a hundred survivors to pile into buses, drive for three hours, and hike another hour to a remote village in the Himalayan foothills. I was all decked out in hiking boots and polypropylene pants, wide brimmed hat and water bottle. I am sure I looked quite ridiculous, struggling up the steep mountainsides in my expedition gear, trying not to pant as the girls swanned past effortlessly in their saris and kitten heels.

"This cough sure makes it hard to climb these mountains!" I exclaimed robustly, as if I was fit enough to hike these slopes without gasping for air under normal circumstances. If any of those good people were unconvinced, they kindly kept it to themselves.

The village was a series of humble bungalows spread out over the rocky soil, which people had dug into terraces for farming. We split into small groups, and I joined a group of four survivors who went door to door sharing their stories with village mothers and daughters. They explained that young girls needed to be careful, how girls could protect themselves from trafficking, and what really happens when you are sold into a brothel, dispelling the 'Pretty Woman' myth that many villagers had been tricked into believing. In a country with such stigma attached to prostitution, the courage of those young women to tell their personal stories was profoundly inspiring.

The villagers seemed greatly surprised by what the girls were telling them, and grateful for the information. To the few who were literate, mostly children, the survivors gave printed information. For everyone else, they posted cartoon-illustrated posters all over the village, depicting human trafficking and its tragic outcome.

The village had been selected for this outreach campaign because girls there had been disappearing, almost certainly trafficked to India. Fifteen to twenty Nepali girls are trafficked every day across the thousand-mile border to India, to Calcutta, Mumbai, Delhi, and sometimes the Middle East.

Seeing the barrenness and poverty of this village made it easier for me to understand how people could be driven to such extremes. There was no work. The soil was inhospitable. The stress of barely surviving year in and year out, the complete lack of options, was sobering.

Some families sell daughters out of absolute desperation. They don't know how bad it will be for their girls. They are so poor that keeping their children home may be life-endangering. In other cases, unscrupulous neighbors or relatives sell girls to traffickers. Sometimes, young men come to the village and marry girls, only to sell them to a brothel in India and repeat the process time after time in other villages.

After a few hours, we assembled in the village square, and the girls performed street theater for a crowd of children two hundred deep, sitting on the ground in rapt attention. I felt sure none of those children would forget the message they heard that day for a long time to come. At the end of the performance, we served up a hot meal to everyone in the village and drove back to Kathmandu as night fell.

A few days later, the police brought a recently arrested trafficker to the shelter so that he could be photographed for the shelter's records, so that the legal team could interview him, and (off the record) so that the girl he had sold could have the opportunity to talk to him.

This young man had sold numerous village girls into brothels after tricking them into false marriages. He cringed in shame as one of his victims, a girl of fifteen, confronted him with the terrible suffering he had caused her. Anuradha Koirala, Maiti Nepal's impassioned founder, less gently took him to task for his wrongdoing. The trafficker looked so young himself - no more than twenty. With his baby face, it was easy to imagine how a young girl would trust him, seeing him as a peer. It was harder to imagine the misery which could compel a young boy to sell naive village girls into a life of slavery.

We left the room to afford them some privacy. Out in the hallway, a mother was waiting to talk to Anuradha. She was a Tamang tribal woman from the countryside, wearing the large earrings and traditional dress of that ethnic group. She had traveled for days to get to Kathmandu, and clutched a photo of her teenage daughter who had disappeared eleven days earlier.

I don't have adequate words to describe the look on that woman's face. She was devoid of expression, yet her eyes managed to convey a vast emptiness which was terrible to behold. Anuradha nodded towards the man accompanying the mother— a husband or uncle. "I am suspecting him," she told us quietly. The man did wear an uncomfortable expression, unreadable to me, but Anuradha had seen it all a thousand times before.

As Anuradha began to interview this bereft family, we stepped outside into a courtyard, and again my reality shifted. In the twilight, a hundred children were singing and dancing exuberantly, some on a raised stage, others on the grass, all laughing and smiling as a teacher led them in a traditional Nepali dance. It was a moment as full of hope and promise as the previous moments were full of loss. It took my breath away.

These experiences prised my heart wide open, and I felt even more urgency to find a way to be of service. The next day, I was given a tremendous gift – the chance to talk with Anuradha, and to ask specifically how I could help her. I expected that she would ask for help with fundraising, or approaching pharmaceutical companies about providing treatment for girls with HIV/AIDS. We had spent time with some of these girls earlier in the day, in the shelter clinic. At that point, Maiti Nepal did not have funding or resources at that time to offer anti-retrovirals, so the girls' lives were cut short, a bitter cruelty after surviving slavery.

I was surprised by the answer Anuradha gave me, which had nothing to do with fundraising or medicine. "Actually... we could use some help finding employment for our older girls," she ventured. "The younger survivors can go back to school. If they get a high school education, or even college, they can rejoin society that way. But some of our older girls are seventeen, eighteen years old or older, and have never even been to kindergarten. It's almost impossible, for them to go back to the beginning. What they need is to be financially independent... but it's hard to find jobs for them here in Nepal".

Trafficking victims are tremendously stigmatized in South Asia. They are blamed for what has been done to them. They are believed to be 'bad girls,' spreading AIDS and bad morals. In this desperately poor, traditional country, the stigma is almost impossible to overcome. Job options are limited for women, even without such extreme obstacles. I remembered, earlier in the day, we had seen thousands of people lined up on the street, standing crowded in line for eight hours to apply for construction jobs in Korea.

Without a job and an income, Anuradha went on, the survivors' futures would always be precarious. A few might be able to marry, but the 'shame' of their past would put them in a vulnerable position in their new family. Even without this added burden, a traditional Nepali marriage is quite oppressive. Each night, the wife is expected to wash her husband's feet, then dip her hands in his dirty foot water and put the water in her mouth, symbolizing her deference to her husband.

Some rescued girls are eventually able to return to their home villages, if their families agree to accept them back. But always the shadow of prostitution follows them, keeping them isolated and vulnerable.

With such disheartening options, many rescued women end up drifting back to the brothels, either because they are re-trafficked, or by their own volition, seeing no better future for themselves. Good, solid, well-paid employment could change this, Anuradha maintained.

In Nepal, in America and throughout the world, women need economic independence to get out of abusive situations. Without their own means of support, they will always be vulnerable.

For several hours, we discussed options for survivor employment, such as sending girls for training as chefs, accountants, or computer programmers. In that first conversation, we didn't come up with a solution. Our ideas were not cost-efficient or practical. We decided to keep thinking about the problem. For me, that amounted to ruminating, by day and in the middle of the night. Fortunately, an answer was not long in coming.

The next day, walking through of the shelter, we came across a room piled high with colorful bags and beaded jewelry. A ray of sunlight was shining through a window and reflecting on the beaded necklaces, causing them to twinkle and glow. The twinkling beads were like a beacon: Here was one answer to the survivor employment issue - beautiful products the women already knew how to create. I realized with a frisson of excitement that these women might already have the skill and means to support themselves. We just had to find a market for their talents.

"These products are a dime a dozen in Nepal," Anuradha said with a sigh. "The girls make them for art therapy, but we haven't been able to sell them".

Looking at the pile of handicrafts and hearing Anuradha's words, the ghost of an idea began to emerge. We could sell the survivors' handicrafts in America, and use them to educate Americans about the issue of trafficking. The next day, I bought $300 of samples, as much as I could fit into two large duffel bags purchased for this purpose.

By the end of the trip, I was missing own kids painfully. I had never been away from them for more than a few nights, and here I had been gone for eleven days. It was time to go home, but I was so grateful for all the experiences, and the insights I had gained in Nepal. I had seen things I never could have imagined, and been profoundly changed. My life was about to take off in yet another entirely new direction and I could feel it bubbling inside me. I was so full of energy, it was impossible to contain myself. I could sense that my excited-puppy energy was getting on everyone's nerves. I could not wait to get home and get to work.

5 FLASHLIGHT

An Indian folktale tells of a young boy who has to walk three miles to another village, late at night. The boy is frightened because it is dark and the way is treacherous. His grandfather gives him a lantern (in modern versions a flashlight).

'Grandfather, it is three miles to the next village! I can only see three feet ahead with this flashlight!'

'Just start walking. Walk those three feet and then you will see another three,' the grandfather tells him. *'That is the only way forward'*

When I got home from Nepal, I was fired up with more energy than I have ever felt in my life, ready to jump into immediate action. Images from the trip were seared into my memory – the Tamang mother and her crumpled Polaroid, the anger and confusion of the fifteen-year-old confronting her trafficker 'husband', the babies bred as human chains to keep their mothers enslaved, their tiny hands joined in a Namaste. These powerful memories added fuel to my fire, propelling me forward, though I still wasn't exactly sure how to get where I wanted to go.

It took nine more months to come up with a solid plan and galvanize support. At this point, my kids were still small, and a lot of my day was taken up with parenting. In the evenings, John and I brainstormed and debated how best to help survivors and shelters.

Our goal was to create jobs that would pay enough for survivors to leave the shelters and support themselves independently, not living on the verge of poverty, but comfortably. We wanted to create opportunities for survivors to enjoy a decent quality of life, and to leave the deprivations of the past behind once and for all. We wanted to get them out of the lowest class of society, where they would always be vulnerable to exploitation. We wanted to help them become slavery-proof.

We mapped out a business model for self-sustaining survivor businesses. The sale of the women's bags and jewelry would generate profit which would cover the costs of the program. The more we sold, the more could expand, hiring and training more survivors. We would provide training to the women so they could become master craftspeople and designers. We planned to offer them other tools - awareness about human and legal rights, leadership and entrepreneurship training – so they could manage and own their own small businesses as the project evolved.

Of course, there were a few bumps in the road during that planning period. (*When aren't there?!*) Soon after returning from my trip, I scheduled a film screening of 'The Day my God Died' at my church. I invited all of my friends and acquaintances, and posted flyers all over town. I was so excited for my community to see the film that had so changed my life. Perhaps others would be similarly inspired.

It didn't work out that way. Other than the small group of churchgoers attending a scheduled service that night, only one person attended my screening. It was embarrassing. Even my closest friends did not come. I felt discouraged that my first public effort was such a failure.

I went home to commiserate with John. "How can people not want to see a film about such an important topic?" I grumbled, with a smidge of self-righteousness. How soon had I forgotten my own reluctance to see the very same film at Tribeca.

John was not one bit sympathetic. "They don't want to see it because they don't want to see it," he shrugged… "People don't want to pay a babysitter and spend their date night seeing a film about sexually exploited kids. Big surprise. You just have to figure out what they *do* want to do, and then use that to get them in the door. Instead of feeling sorry for yourself, you should just learn from the experience and adjust your game plan. The key to success in any business is to be flexible".

This was solid business advice. If you plan on doing something ambitious, plan for lots of things to go wrong along the way. As the old saying goes, 'Failure is not the opposite of success. It's part of it'. Plan for regular disappointment. Taking risks and failing are a necessary part of the process, and not something to be feared.

In this case, I learned that I needed to adjust my game plan. Apparently, most people don't want to see tragic documentaries or hear lectures on human rights atrocities. They do want to drink wine (or tea), eat cheese (or chocolate), hang out with friends, and if they are women, shop for cute gifts. In a safe and comfortable setting, I realized, people would likely be more open to learning about horrific gender violence.

We developed the idea of selling our survivor-made products at home parties, educating people in an uplifting and hopeful manner. These 'Awareness Parties' ended up being an essential part of getting our organization off the ground.

Raising awareness was essential because the issue and even the term 'human trafficking' was largely unknown at that time. When I told people I was working on the issue of human trafficking, they would often say, "You mean drug trafficking?" or even "You mean people that have been in traffic accidents?" Sometimes they would just look confused and overwhelmed and wander off in search of lighter conversation.

Over the next nine months, I continued to work with Friends of Maiti Nepal, and also worked intensively on this new idea. At first, I hoped to be able to do the project under the umbrella of Friends of Maiti Nepal, but when I proposed it to Joe and Brigitte, they felt that it was too much of a diversion from their core mission. Although I could understand their point, I was disappointed. I agonized for ages about going off in this new direction on my own. John eventually became annoyed because I wanted to talk it through all the time.

I so enjoyed being part of a team, and wasn't sure I had the skills yet to run my own agency. I didn't want to be one of those people who have to do everything their own way. And I had promised to help Friends of Maiti Nepal. I was grateful for the opportunity and had no desire to ditch out on the effort. Still, this new idea had captured my imagination and I felt strongly that it could work. After a while, it seemed that Joe and Brigitte did not need as much help from me. Perhaps they too were moving in a different direction. In any case, it felt like an appropriate time to move on.

Letting go and moving on are always hard for me. I've been forced to let go of a lot of things and even people since I began doing this work, but I haven't gotten one bit better at it. Really, how could I? My work is all about holding on, reclaiming that which has been let go. You can't be good at everything.

Once I made the decision to forge ahead and create a new organization, I scheduled a meeting for people interested in the issue, and posted flyers around town. We held our first meeting at a local coffee shop. I was delighted when six people showed up. We decided to host an auction to raise money to buy more products made by. The night of the auction, there was a snowstorm, and we had less than twenty guests, but still raised over $2000.

John and I chipped in another $3000, giving me a total of $5000 to buy our first order. We applied for nonprofit status and chose a name for our new baby: Made By Survivors (which was later reanamed Her Future Coalition). I didn't have everything figured out yet, but I had a plan for the next few months. Our project was still experimental, but we were doing it, not just talking about it.

I had my flashlight and was on my way.

6 WHEN THINGS GO WRONG

"What do you mean the Nepali government has just been overthrown?! I am supposed to going to Nepal the week after next!" I raged, aware that my outburst was unlikely to affect international affairs in the slightest.

I had planned my second trip to Nepal, one year after my first visit. Now that trip was just weeks away, I had my ticket, and I was starting to think about what to pack. I planned to visit Maiti Nepal and pick up a motherlode of products, and to make arrangements for shipping home whatever I couldn't carry.

Then one morning my plans came to a screeching halt. The king of Nepal overthrew his own parliament in a coup, and the country was thrown into total confusion. Flights in and out of Nepal were suspended. Phone, power, and Internet communication were cut off. Clearly, my trip was going to have to wait. The State Department advised strenuously against travel to Nepal.

I worried that the country would be thrown into long term chaos. Nepal had already been destabilized for fifteen years by Maoist guerrillas, and this was one factor in the trafficking problem getting so out of hand. Law enforcement resources had been diverted for years to fight the Maoists. The economy was devastated by the insurgency as well. In addition to my concern for the safety of the girls at the shelter and all the Nepali people, I had the very personal problem that my plan was no longer feasible. I indulged in a few moments of despair and panic, and attempted to take a deep cleansing breath.

When that failed, I called John, who calmly went online and researched anti-trafficking groups in countries other than Nepal. He found one in Cambodia, Hagar International, that looked promising.

Then we found AFESIP, a shelter and employment program for survivors in Cambodia, and Mirror Foundation, a prevention program in Northern Thailand. We emailed the groups, and all three responded quickly that they were interested in meeting with me.

I rescheduled my trip for the following month, with an itinerary that now included Thailand and Cambodia, with five days in Nepal at the very end (hoping it would be was safe by then to travel there). Joe and Brigitte reassured me that I could easily walk the two miles to the airport from the shelter if there was a 'bandh' (general strike imposed by the Maoists) and suggested I bring a rolling suitcase in case of this eventuality.

Although I had always imagined that we would partner with many shelter homes in the future, the overthrow of Nepal forced me to make this decision much sooner than expected, and this proved to be very advantageous. The handicrafts that I bought from the Cambodian and Thai groups added beauty and diversity to our collection, giving us a more successful first year that we would have otherwise had.

Things fall apart all the time in this work. Sometimes they come back together even better and stronger than before. I used to get really disheartened or fly into a panic when things went wrong, but in many cases, what seemed to be disasters later led to breakthroughs. Something unexpected and wonderful has often risen from the ashes of a disappointment.

My second trip to Asia was another revelation, at times a brutal one. It deepened my insight into gender violence and strengthened my conviction to help people escape from slavery and remain free, to take control of their own lives so they were less vulnerable.

In Nepal, I had spent my time at the shelter, and at one awareness campaign in the countryside. In Cambodia, I went into the red light districts for the first time. I spent my days with street children who were sold for sexual exploitation to tourists, and everywhere I saw pretty teenagers on the arms of middle-aged male tourists, and young girls smiling in the doorways of brothels, their eyes cold and hard as granite.

My heart broke in fifty places during that trip. I forgave myself for my initial reluctance, at Tribeca Film Festival, to see a documentary about child trafficking. Seeing children suffering so acutely was excruciating. No wonder people try to avoid it. The problem is that when we don't allow ourselves to witness people being hurt, we aren't doing anything to stop it either. Now that I had taken myself to the front lines, I had no choice but to see. Over time, I would develop heavier emotional armor, so I wouldn't be so easily distressed by the girls' suffering, but on this first trip, I was surprised by how painful it was.

The trip actually started on a high note. A friend who was a flight attendant gave me a companion pass, and I got to fly first class all the way to Bangkok for just a few hundred dollars. That was one of the best days of my life - glasses of fine wine, lying flat out to sleep, and Haagen Dazs ice cream in porcelain bowls. There was a brief slump in Tokyo, when it looked like there was no space on the flight to Bangkok, but ultimately I made the connection and arrived in Bangkok at 3:00 am. By the time I checked into my hotel, I was disoriented and ravenously hungry.

I ordered sticky rice and mango, a dessert dish, from room service. About halfway through eating it, I realized that I was literally moaning in pleasure. As I recall, it was tasty, but sticky rice is a simple dish and I had eaten it before without such intense appreciation. I have never before or since enjoyed a plate of food more than that plate of sticky rice. It was late, I was hungry, and above all, I was so grateful to have arrived, to be in Asia ready to launch my new project, and to be a free woman in a nice hotel who could order food at 3:00 am if she was hungry. I was a woman with choices, who hopefully would be able to do something to offer that same freedom and choice to others.

A short but sweet five hours later, I was back at the airport, flying to the small city of Chiang Rai in the northernmost part of Thailand, near the Burmese border. The Hill tribe people who live in the mountains of this region have neither Thai nor Burmese citizenship. This problem, along with their minority status, grinding poverty, lack of education and jobs, and history of violent persecution makes the young girls of the region exceptionally vulnerable to trafficking.

Families in the region had been selling their daughters for as little as $150. Traffickers would first sell the girls' virginity at a local hotel. This heinous practice allows men to buy a young virgin and to use and abuse her for several days or sometimes as long as a week. The trauma these girls endure is made worse by their isolation. When this nightmare finally ends, the girls are sent to brothels in faraway cities, from which many never return. One agency working on the problem in the region was the Mirror Foundation, and I hoped to find a way to help them.

Alas, things did not get off to a smooth start. I was supposed to be met at my hotel by a representative of Mirror Foundation, and driven out to their center forty-five minutes from the city. Our meeting was scheduled for 9:00 a.m. I stood hopefully on the hotel steps for half an hour, but still no one came. By 9:30, I was becoming anxious. Traveling in Asia, the issue of trafficking, and running my own nonprofit were all so new to me. I felt slightly inadequate and extremely awkward, pacing outside my hotel waiting in vain for someone to meet me. It was hot and ridiculously humid. My hair was soon hanging in limp strands.

The doorman offered to call my contact at Mirror Foundation on his mobile phone. It was then that I realized, to my great chagrin, that I had not written down the name of my contact, nor did I have any phone number for him to call. All of this information was stored in my laptop, but the batteries had run out during the long flight to Thailand and I had no adaptor to recharge it.

Bad moment.

Deep Cleansing Breath (failed)

My heart constricted. It would be a colossal waste of time and money to come all the way to Chiang Rai for nothing. My loved ones know that I lose my keys and wallet with alarming regularity, but this no time for such carelessness. I was alone in rural Thailand with a job to do. I managed to jury-rig an electrical adaptor (the expression 'fitting in a square peg into a round hole' comes to mind), plugged in my laptop, and found the name – Lawan - and email address of my contact. I sent Lawan an email but had no confidence that she would check her email in time.

The doorman tried to look up the phone number for Mirror Foundation. Thankfully, he was persistent because it took forty-five nerve-wracking minutes and many phone calls to other agencies before he finally tracked them down. My heart was practically pounding out of my chest by the time we got through to Lawan at 11:00. She was gratifyingly sorry for the mix-up (I think she had completely forgotten our appointment) and immediately dispatched a tuk-tuk (kind of like a dune buggy with three wheels and two-stroke engine) to pick me up and bring me to the center. I was much relieved because by that point, I was extremely stressed out, and feeling like a complete loser, and this was still only the first day of my trip.

My tuk-tuk ride, though noisy, bumpy and reeking of diesel, was a pleasant way to see the Thai countryside, which was lush and beautiful as a postcard. I found it hard to imagine anything ugly happening in such an idyllic place. The tuk-tuk carried me up to the tiny village of Huoy Kuom where I met with the staff of Mirror Foundation and spent an informative afternoon learning about the hill tribes and their vulnerability to human trafficking. There are several different tribes in the region, including big-ears Karen, whose women wear giant earrings to stretch their earlobes, long-neck Karen, whose women stretch their necks with stacks of chokers, the Akha, the Lisu and the Hmong. All have rich and unique cultures and a long history of discrimination and poverty.

For some Hill Tribe families, selling a daughter can make the difference between barely making it and total destitution. In other cases, you can see which family in the village has sold a daughter by their shiny new roof or TV set. I learned that in some areas, girls are actually 'bred' for prostitution, with pretty girls pre-selected at a young age. Local people had begun noticing a few years earlier that there were fewer and fewer teenage girls in their villages. They would see the little girls until they were ten or eleven. Then overnight the girl children would disappear.

Several agencies sprung up in the area to address the crisis, including Mirror Foundation. The handicrafts the women were making at their center were outstanding. I bought practically the entire stock they had on hand.

Later that night, back in Chiang Rai, I enjoyed some quiet time reflecting on the day's experiences. I was learning so much, digging deeper into the issue, talking to women about their needs, their dreams and challenges. I felt optimistic about our project and the positive impact it could have.

7 HOLLOW EYES

"Talking is well and good, but in order to really understand the flesh trade, you have to see for yourself," said Ana. "How about I pick you up tonight, on my motor scooter, and show you some of the red light areas?"

It was my first night in Cambodia, which is where to go if you need to see the worst child trafficking and exploitation anywhere in the world. Stark billboards at the airport and in all the tourist areas warned Americans, '*Abuse a child in this country, Go to Jail in Yours!*'

Between 1970 and 1980, a decade of war, genocide and man-made famine wiped out over half of Cambodia's population, and pulverized the country's infrastructure. It was still only partly reconstructed. During the 'Pol Pot Time,' as Cambodians refer to it, people were forced to turn against their neighbors and family members, causing a complete breakdown within the society and a lingering fear and distrust. This, along with extreme poverty, fuels the sex tourism industry, which devours tens of thousands of Cambodian girls every year, including very young children.

I always to keep it positive, but on this visit to Cambodia, it was difficult to do so.

Thankfully my gloom was tempered by the inspiration I got from the anti-trafficking organizations I met in Cambodia, AFESIP and Hagar International. Both groups were rescuing girls from forced prostitution, giving them shelter care, education, counseling, and jobs. A woman who earns a good salary is respected in Cambodia; people are willing to turn a blind eye to her past to some extent. Without help and interventions like these, trafficking victims in Cambodia are blamed and stigmatized for what has been done to them, sometimes by the very families that sold or sent them into prostitution.

In Cambodia as in Nepal and other countries in the region, many parents send their children into trafficking unknowingly, tricked by traffickers or neighbors or relatives into believing their children would be doing domestic or other labor, not forced into prostitution. They accept a risky proposition because the situation in the home is so desperate. For their child to continue living at home may itself be life-threatening when there isn't enough food to go around. A small chance for a better life is better than no chance at all, they reason. By the time they realize their child is never coming back, it's already too late.

A smaller number of families sell their children into slavery for financial gain, knowing the true nature of the situation. In some communities, selling daughters has become normalized.

Many trafficked children come from refugee communities (such as the Vietnamese in Cambodia) or tribal groups who are excluded from mainstream society and sometimes do not have full citizenship. Extreme poverty and limited legal rights drive these families into desperate decisions.

On the morning of my first day in Phhom Penh, I met with Ana Chico, a young Spanish woman who was the co-director of AFESIP Fair Fashion, a sewing and tailoring employment program for survivors of sex trafficking. Near the end of our meeting, she surprised me with an offer of a tour of the red light areas - on her motor scooter.

I was torn between gratitude, for Ana's willingness to spend her evening showing me sex slavery up close, and profound apprehension. I had heard some truly horrendous stories from her already. I felt like my shell was dangerously close to cracking as it was. And now we were going straight into the heart of darkness.

At night. On a motor scooter.

That afternoon, I met with another outstanding organization, Hagar International, which was employing survivors in a dairy business and also making stylish totes and backpacks from recycled rice bags.

After visiting Hagar, I walked around the city for a few hours, then went back to my hotel room and tried to relax. I was surprisingly apprehensive about the evening to come. Riding around on tiny Ana's tiny Vespa seemed like a foolish idea to begin with, on these crazy streets. Eight or ten lanes of traffic were crammed into a space designed for three. And, I knew we would be riding that scooter to places full of horrendous suffering, places that it would hurt to see.

It was uncomfortably hot and humid, and my hotel did not have air conditioning. I took a cold shower and lay under the listless fan, worrying. I was in way over my head. I also knew there was only one way to get my head back above water and that was to stare down my fear, open my heart, and learn everything I possibly could.

My hotel was itself a charitable venture. The staff were former street kids. Beautiful foliage and bamboo furniture gave the feeling of an olde-world oasis. However, the the hotel was located directly across from the Toul Sleng Genocide Museum, a torture facility which has been left exactly as it was in the days of the Khmer Rouge. All day long, calm, happy tourists entered the museum, and emerged later in a state of absolute distress - crying, staggering, holding their heads in their hands. Watching their reactions from my hotel room window only increased my anxiety about the evening to come. Was that what I was going to look like by the end of the night?

At 8:00, Ana showed up on her little scooter. I'm 5'10" and solidly built, but somehow we managed to fit companionably on the small vehicle. Ana turned out to be a skillful driver, quite up to the challenge of navigating the streets of Phnom Penh. She first drove us out to Tuol Kork, a pot-holed dirt road bordered by dozens of tin sheds. These were brothels frequented mostly by local men. Teenage girls stood out front advertising the brothel's services, and inside, girls serviced customers in small, filthy cubicles for about a dollar. The younger girls - those that have recently been brought to the brothel and are undergoing a seasoning period where they are kept locked up - were not out on this main street. Ana told me that those kids were kept hidden in smaller alleyways off the main road.

Next we rode down to the Mekong River waterfront area, to a park where pedophiles go to buy street children for the night. The area is populated by homeless families, and the many boys and girls selling books and cards to tourists are easy picking for every kind of exploitation.

All over the city in hotels and bars, Western and Asian tourists were cavorting with pretty young teenagers. Some of these men were pretending to have a girlfriend for a few days, a totally powerless girlfriend who could be made to do anything they wanted. Western clients usually prefer to pretend they are out on a date, Ana explained, taking the girls out for drinks or dinner, pretending there is a 'special connection' between them. The hollow look in the eyes of these teenagers, despite their practiced smiles, made a mockery of this pretense. Apparently the guys didn't notice.

The girls were pretending to be having a good time, and perhaps the clients are able to convince themselves it was true. The bars and clubs where girls are trafficked have become experts at making it fast, easy and socially acceptable for these men to do something many would never dare do at home. Girls were dancing in cages with numbers around their necks, and the clients could just order up their chosen girl by her number. Is there a more potent metaphor for powerlessness than a number slung around a girl's neck?

We went into one of the bars, and Ana told me a story of an event she had witnessed there a few days earlier. "An American guy was negotiating with the Mama-San to buy a girl for the night. She brought out all these beautiful young girls, one after the other, but he just kept shaking his head and saying 'younger'. Finally the mama-san brought out this really young kid, twelve or thirteen at the most. The customer looked her up and down, made her spin around in a circle, and then he reached out and grabbed her breast, and roughly nodded. He didn't even buy her a drink. He just led her upstairs. She looked so scared".

Ana looked desolated as she told this story. "I didn't know what to do," she admitted. I could find no words to comfort her.

After visiting some of the bars, we drove past a huge crumbling apartment complex, a place infamous for the selling of virgins. The cost to buy a girl's virginity in this ruinous place was $50 to $300. According to Ana, men from Japan and other wealthier Asian countries sometimes come to Cambodia to celebrate major business deals by having sex with virgins. There is also a belief in parts of Asia that having sex with a virgin can cure you of AIDS, so some men seek virgins for this purpose.

I considered breaking down a door, grabbing some girls and making a run for it, but decided that would probably not lead to long term, systemic change, and might instead lead to my ending up beaten and bloody in an alleyway.

I went back to my hotel feeling physically ill and totally depressed. I had to admit that I had come to Cambodia supremely unprepared. I saw myself, in that moment, as a well-meaning but clearly delusional suburban mom with no resources to combat this evil. I wondered if I would be able to keep going with this work, and even if I should.

But what choice did I have? After seeing that crumbling ruin -those young girls trained to giggle and smile as their dreams are trodden to dust by a series of careless tourists - there was no way I could turn away. In the face of such evil, there is nothing to do but fight it, however and wherever you can.

I called John. He advised me to stay focused on the job at hand, and not allow myself to get bogged down in all the pain and ugliness. "That will only paralyze you", he advised. "You can deal with your feelings later, when you get home. For now, just do the job you went there to do".

This was good advice, because of course this was just the first of many hard times along this journey. Where things are truly broken – as in the case of child sex trafficking – it takes time, patience, and an enormous force of will to make any kind of significant change.

To heal any corner of the world, you have to be willing to feel other people's pain, and perhaps to take some of their burden onto yourself. You feel despair. You keep going. You screw up (like I did in Chiang Rai, and many other times). You keep going. Nothing seems to be working, you get burned out. Take a break, get some fresh air, love on yourself until you feel better, and get back to it. You don't know how to do what you need to do. Ask for help and keep going. People let you down. They give up on themselves or try to tear you down. Just keep moving forward.

In time, a barren field will become a beautiful garden. A person who seemed wounded beyond repair will be restored. In the most desperate situations, when I feel like I have little to offer, at least I have this:

I'm still here.

8 ONWARDS AND UPWARDS

I'm happy to report that the following day was much better, a welcome contrast from my nighttime visit to the underworld. We left early for the two-hour drive to the village of Kompong Cham, where the AFESIP workshop is located. We started the journey on Ana's scooter, but then (thank heaven!), graduated to a car.

We were joined by Rotha, Ana's co-director at AFESIP Fair Fashion, and two young girls. One was a survivor in her early twenties who had trained as a tailor and was now ready to join the team at the workshop. The other was a child survivor, ten years of age, who was going to live at the AFESIP orphanage. The younger girl had never been in a car before, and as the road was very bumpy, she was repeatedly carsick. This is common for people who have never ridden in cars, I learned. In between the vomiting and stopping to clean up, the older girl made beautiful origami creatures for me out of the small bills in my wallet. The five of us were a merry party, in spite of everything.

At some point we stopped at a roadside stand to eat. Guidebooks advise strenuously against eating at roadside stands, but apparently I am protected by some powerful angels, or just a large population of healthy enteric bacteria, because I always dig in to whatever is on offer, and I have only once had a digestive problem in Asia.

We ordered some Cokes, which surprisingly, the shopkeeper decanted into sandwich-sized plastic bags. Then he inserted into each bag a straw, and sealed the whole contraption with a rubber band. Apparently they keep the glass bottles and recycle them for the deposit. It was low-tech, but effective.

The Coke, though warm and bizarrely presented, was one of the most refreshing beverage experiences of my life. As with the sticky rice a few days earlier, I was experiencing all of life more intensely than I had in years. I appreciated things more, maybe because they weren't always so readily available, or because the majority of people around me did not have even their most basic needs met. Being in that environment was changing my perspective.

The night before, I had hit a low point, but now I was almost giddy with hope. Despite the circumstances which make Ana and Rotha's project necessary, they are in the business of hope, and their mood was equally jovial. When we arrived in the village, it was easy to see why they were so happy to get there.

Forty young women awaited us at the workshop, buzzing with excitement. The space was bright, and airy, a proper setting for people to work, create and heal. After a long, warm welcome, the girls went back to their work, still laughing and smiling all the while. They were in the middle of filling a large order of silk clothing for a buyer in Spain.

Rotha explained that the presence of these survivors in the village was initially not welcomed. The villagers blamed the women for the abuse that was done to them. They believed that these were 'bad girls', who would spread AIDS and low morals to the young people of the village.

However, women that earn a living also earn respect in Cambodian society, and the womens' high wages, along with their fine character, led to a gradual acceptance by the villagers. Several young women had recently gotten married, rented houses, and started families, further integrating into the village community.

The best part of my day was sitting on the floor with the girls while we ate lunch, sharing in their day, not as a donor or buyer, but simply as a friend. I like to be among the girls, on the same level, not apart from them, or looming over them. That's why I always join the girls sitting on the floor, even if it gives me a cramp after a while.

I was surprised by how loving and open these young women were. Naturally they were a bit shy and reticent at first, but if I approached them gently, first making eye contact, then smiling, then allowing them to initiate physical contact – such as holding my hand or offering a hug – I soon felt warmly accepted.

What I really wanted was to stay at that workshop for weeks or months, and not to be a visitor at all, but a permanent fixture. I longed to mother those girls, to hug them close, listen to their sorrows and dreams, and offer my shoulder to cry on. I yearned to give those girls the love and family they had been denied in childhood.

This wasn't possible (yet) because I had a whole other life with two small children and a husband back home. For the time being, supporting the survivors' livelihoods from the U.S. was the best way for me to contribute to their healing. Sitting on the floor with them for one afternoon was as close as I could get.

One of the girls, Srey, had recently been promoted to team captain because of her commitment and skill. She sat me down and showed me every one of the designs the team was making, proudly pointing out the reinforced seams and delicate embroidery. Srey had been trafficked into a brothel along with her little sister, before the age of ten. Her confidence and strength astonished me. Meeting girls like Srey, who have suffered in ways that are difficult to even imagine, yet who remain so joyous, so loving, and so hopeful for the future, is inspiring and at the same time, humbling. It's hard to justify complaining about *anything* after meeting them.

Later in the afternoon, we dropped off the little girl who had driven in our car to the orphanage for child survivors in the same village. The youngest survivor at the orphanage was only three, which was terribly hard to comprehend. Seeing these tiny children playing and doing their schoolwork was incongruous with the knowledge that they were all survivors of sex trafficking. Every one of them had been rescued from a brothel or from child marriage.

I remembered John's words, and put my feelings on hold, to deal with at a later time. This is a necessary skill which I have since perfected. No one wants to be an object of pity, and it does no good to fall apart, or start crying or to appear shocked in the face of people who have been victimized. That only makes them feel worse about their circumstances.

The orphanage staff was loving and the atmosphere tranquil. The children were all behaving normally. None seemed angry, violent or catatonic, as I would have expected after what they had been through.

Ana and I borrowed some bikes to tour the village and meet other community members. It was excruciatingly hot and humid out there in the jungle. I was told not to venture off the road for any reason because there were still many live land mines. The bike riding was a little awkward because I was wearing a Cambodian split trouser/skirt that kept flying up in a most immodest fashion. At least this provided comic relief to my companion, and to any villagers who witnessed it.

I loved that whole day in Kompong Cham, talking to the girls, learning about their goals and challenges, choosing fabrics for our order, and seeing the survivors creating something beautiful - in the workshop, in the village and in the world. That day came just when I needed it most. The night before I had felt so overwhelmed with the suffering I was witnessing, and frustrated with my inability to fix it, that I seriously wondered if I would be able to continue. By the time we got back to the city from Kompong Cham late that second night, I was as sweaty and dusty as I have ever been in my life, but also full of hope.

I flew on to Nepal the next morning. My route to the airport took me right past the crumbling ruin where young girls are sold as virgins. I had been on an emotional roller-coaster the whole time I was in Cambodia: hopeful... morose; inspired... devastated; reinvigorated... eviscerated. I'm sure Cambodia has many cultural wonders (all of which I had failed to see on this trip), but after seeing its dark underside, I was spiritually fatigued, and frankly, glad to be leaving. Once on the airplane, I closed my eyes and for once, did not bother to choke back or even wipe away my tears.

It felt great to get back to the low-key vibe and cooler temperatures of Nepal. I spent several days at Maiti Nepal, and also found another partner agency, in which women made paper from renewable resources. The women in that group come from the Dalit, or 'Untouchable', caste, and are vulnerable to trafficking and every other kind of exploitation. The caste system, which dates back centuries, is a rigid social classification system which determines what kind of jobs people can hold (highest: priest, lowest: cleaning up human waste or handling garbage, leather, or dead bodies). Caste also dictates what people should eat, who they can marry, and their place in society.

All societies, including ours in the West, have class systems, based on income, skin color, or family background. The difference is that in traditional South Asian societies, it is impossible to rise above your caste. Dalits do not have even the most basic human rights, despite laws passed in 1962 which outlawed the caste system.

The Dalit women described childhoods in which their neighbors carried spray bottles to cleanse themselves after coming into accidental contact with them. To this day, the women and girls in their communities are often raped by men of higher castes, crimes which are rarely prosecuted. I found it hard to imagine what that kind of treatment, day after day, year after year, would do to a person's sense of self-worth. For Dalit people, the belief that they are worthless has been ingrained in them since birth. This makes it easy to exploit and enslave them.

Near the end of my trip, I was strolling through Kathmandu's tourist district with my young friend Nilu, who had grown up at Maiti Nepal. We stopped for a coffee at the Big Belly Café. The area was crawling with backpackers and tourists from all over the world, so it was no surprise when an English woman sat down next to us. We said 'hello', and started chatting.

After a few minutes, the woman, whose name was Emma, asked me what I was doing in Kathmandu. "Well, it's a little unusual," I said cautiously. "I'm here buying products made by survivors of sex trafficking, which I plan to sell back home to raise money and awareness". Emma looked stunned, as people usually do, but what she said next was the last thing I expected.

"Snap!" (That's British for 'Me Too!') Out of the seven billion people on the planet, there were probably less than five of us engaged in that particular activity at that moment in time. And yet two of us met in a cafe in Kathmandu. It was wildly unlikely, a crazy coincidence or perhaps, a small miracle to help me on my way.

Like me, Emma was just starting to launch her project. She was in Kathmandu buying products from another shelter for survivors. Her group was rescuing and caring for kids who had been trafficked into Indian circuses. In the circus, the children were forced to perform dangerous stunts without safety nets, deliberately malnourished to delay development, and subjected to regular physical and sexual abuse. In fact, many of the circuses are little more than traveling brothels, in which the girls are exploited in 'private shows'.

It was so encouraging to meet someone on the same path, and over the years, Emma and I shared ideas, lamented failures, and learned from each other's experiences. A few years later, when we were in a tight spot financially, Emma donated $4000 from a fundraising event, which saved the day. The year before that, we helped her pick up the pieces when one of her programs imploded. That chance meeting at the Big Belly Café was just one of the many small miracles which have helped me along this journey.

I flew home the next day weighed down with such an enormous amount of luggage (stuffed with survivor-made products), that I needed two luggage carts to manage it. It was a wonder they let me on the airplane. When I started explaining the situation to the customs officer in New York, he just shook his head and waved me through, duty-free.

I came back from that trip with a lot more than two hundred pounds of bags and jewelry. I came back with a deeper knowledge of the issue, and with renewed confidence and energy. Employment was one of the things survivors needed most. For the first time, I felt not just that we had to find a way to improve the lives of survivors, but that we could.

9 KEEPING CALM AND CARRYING ON

Back home, I laid out a huge pile of handicrafts on the floor of my spare room. The pieces were exquisite and unique. The story behind them was compelling. I bundled the various products into sets. I made a cup of tea and brought it upstairs to drink. Then I realized with an unpleasant jolt that I had no idea what to do next!

More tea. When the second cup did not offer the epiphany I'd hoped for, I succumbed to a mild panic. I had taken steps A, B, and C without a concrete plan for D-Z. I would have to sleep on it.

One good night's sleep and no new ideas later, I drove to Barnes and Noble and picked up the 'Idiot's Guide to Import/Export". I had no experience with import, or with running a retail business. In my whole life, I had only worked for four years at a 'real' job, having mostly been a self-employed musician and then a mother and self-employed musician.

Despite my lack of experience, my recent trip had intensified my belief that the survivors couldn't wait. Sometimes I got lucky and people with more expertise showed up to help. One of the suggestions from my 'Idiot's Guide to Import/Export' was to get a customs broker. Not knowing how to select one, I randomly called Will Francis and signed a contract with him to clear our shipments through customs. The following day, Will called me back. "I'm sorry," he said. "I have to revise the quote I gave you yesterday". I sighed inwardly, hoping this was not going to get too much more expensive. "I read through the information you sent me," he said, "and actually, I am going to donate my services. The cost of each customs clearance will now be… completely free".

Will's spontaneous and generous response was so encouraging. This work has consistently brought me into contact with the finest and best elements of the human spirit. Of course, the work is necessary because of some people's heinous acts against others. Still, the darker the places you go, the brighter your own light can shine. Where there has been no love or kindness, the smallest act of love is transforming.

I emailed Andy Levine, the filmmaker who created 'The Day My God Died'. Andy put a link on the film's website, through which people could sign up to host a home party. When the film aired on PBS, fifty people contacted me about hosting Awareness Parties all over America. Many of my local friends and neighbors also offered to host parties.

Now we had products in hand, we had customs clearance, we had shelters and survivors keen to make more products for us to sell, and we had a venue for selling their products – everything we needed to get started.

That first year running the charity was a magical time when anything seemed possible. Our first Awareness Party took place a month after I returned from Asia, at the home of my friend Raquel. Raquel had promised to invite every socially conscious woman she knew, and she wasn't whistlin' Dixie. There were at least thirty socially conscious women at her party. It was the first opportunity I had to showcase our products, and the cause, to a group of people who did not already know me. It was a gift to be able to share the survivors' stories, and my own experiences for the first time, with such a caring and attentive group.

Raquel's friends were incredibly supportive, and that first party was a big confidence-builder. Financially, it was also a great success. We sold $1600 worth of bags and jewelry. Some of the guests from that first party are volunteers and friends to this day.

For the next nine months, I spoke at Awareness Parties all over New England. Between Thanksgiving to Christmas, I attended seventeen parties. Maya and Luke often came with me, watching cartoons while I told heartbreaking stories of trafficking in the next room. We all ate too many brownies, and laid out our expanding collection of wares in living rooms throughout the region. Meanwhile, volunteers signed up online to host parties all over the country, so when I wasn't Awareness-partying, I was shipping out boxes, or ordering more products from our partners, who were pleasantly surprised by their growing success.

I learned through trial and area that the gruesome details of human trafficking were not appropriate for most people's first exposure to the topic. Horror stories were more likely to paralyze than to galvanize. I learned to leave out the most disturbing details and focus on the resilience and potential of the survivors. If people became interested, they could go online and find out the gory details easily enough.

My strategy evolved to showing people, through a series of stories and facts, that it is possible for every person to make a difference to a terrible problem, that people all over the world are doing so, and that we all can too.

All that year, I worked fiendishly, starting as soon as I dropped the kids at preschool. Then I would work up to the last possible second, and race out the door at 12:30 to pick them up, because the school allowed parents to arrive up to fifteen minutes late without penalty. I was always exactly fifteen minutes late, and gave myself the nickname 'Late Mom', but since I was so consistent in my lateness, I don't think my children ever even realized I was late. They just assumed people got picked up in the same order every day and they were last. If they did notice, they were very forgiving, and have remained so. Our work has shaped Maya and Luke's childhood and values in many wonderful ways.

Happily, I was not doing all this work on my own. Friends stepped up to help, and others became dear friends when they rallied around the cause. The work drew incredible people to us. We set the tone of the organization to be innovative, casual, and joyful.

The issue of slavery, and particularly child sex trafficking, is so devastating that the only way we can cope with it is with love, with humor, and with a spirit of celebration of every small victory. In fact our motto became 'We put the fun back in fundamental human rights'.

Of course, some things did not work out the way I planned. Our biggest problem in the early years was funding, as in the total lack of it. Not just for our project, but for anti-trafficking efforts in general, there was very little grant money available. That first year, I could find no major US foundations with trafficking or slavery as an area of interest. I sent out a series of grant applications to foundations with a focus on women, human rights, and Asia. Unfortunately, I had no experience with grant-writing, and my grant applications bore no fruit whatsoever.

Clearly, this was going to take time, time that some survivors did not have. They needed help immediately, and I was hell-bent on finding a way to give it to them. That is why John and I decided to do something that was either brave or reckless, unconventional or totally insane. We took out the equity from our house and used it to fund the charity ourselves.

It was a risky move and not one that I recommend to everyone. It led to some stress and hard times later. On the other hand, going out on a limb like that gave a big jump-start to our project. It inspired other people to help. It opened the door for some miraculous windfalls later on. It forced us to simplify our lives and it gave us and our children a new appreciation of the many blessings we still had. Our investment in our dream paid off tenfold in the end, if not financially, then in terms of the love and satisfaction it brought to our lives.

In order to make a significant impact in the world, you have to step far out of your comfort zone, whatever that means for you. You might have to give up some things that you thought you needed. At times, it is bound to make you uncomfortable.

10 'TIL DEATH DO US PART

A few months later, I was at serious risk for killing my husband.

As my life had been steadily turned upside down since seeing the documentary two years before, John's life had been changing too. Here's the thing about John and me: we are *really* different. I'm liberal, he's somewhat conservative. I'm spontaneous and assume things will all work out somehow. John is more skeptical and his plans include the worst outcomes as well as the best. I'm diplomatic and conflict-avoiding, while John is blunt, sometimes to the point of rudeness. I was an artist, he was an investment banker, and so on.

Despite our differences, I married John because he always has my back. He has always gotten wholeheartedly behind everything I've done. When I was a musician, he carried the heavy gear, engineered the sound recording, paid for equipment, and built me a home studio plank by plank. We first met in New York City at a music club, and grew close when he began volunteering at the youth program where I worked. I decided I should go out with him when I noticed he was always right beside me, hammer and duct tape in hand, fixing every problem, large or small. If it was raining in the Harlem park where we ran arts workshops, John would whip up a shelter with tarps and scrap metal. *Resourceful,* I noted. *An adoring friend. Easy on the eyes. Why had I not noticed all this before?*

Our friendship deepened, and one New Year's Day, after a rather uninspiring gig with my band (I mean really, who goes out the day *after* New Year's Eve?), I suggested we go back to John's house and watch movies. On a whim, I decided I would casually put my thigh right next to his and see if there was any zing. If there was, we could take our friendship to the next level. If there was no zing, I could just put my arm around his shoulders and give him a friendly squeeze, slap him on the back and wish him a Happy New Year, with no one any the wiser.

As it turned out, there was quite a zing. I kept my thigh where it was. We stayed up all night watching movies, talking and holding hands, and then John asked me on our first real date.

Our romance grew into love, and we probably would soon have gotten engaged, but instead, after long years of trying, my band got a record deal and I went on tour for the next two years. Near the end of those two years, John joined me on tour in Alaska, and proposed at dawn during a noisy and violent bald eagle feeding. *Memorable.*

The first year of running the charity, John was working long hours as an investment banker, and helping me evenings and weekends. Every moment he wasn't working or parenting, he was figuring out logistics, software, or strategy. His brilliant ideas and skills were instrumental to the success of the organization.

However…

Despite my appreciation of his many contributions, I was shocked when John announced his wish to quit his banking job and join me full-time in the charity work. I've never thought of myself as the kind of person who could work with her spouse. In fact, I'd always secretly believed that couples who work together are codependent, or gluttons for punishment, or they just didn't have any other friends with whom to start a business.

My misgivings aside, John was serious about this plan. He had found in this project something more meaningful than any work he had done before, and the challenge of making it succeed was compelling. He no longer felt as inspired in his work as an investment banker, and was ready to chuck in the great salary and perks for a life of simplicity and service. Who could criticize such a gesture? With mixed feelings of admiration and apprehension, I agreed to the plan. Since John had provided much of the funding and technical expertise to get the project off the ground, it was the least I could do.

One evening in October, we went out to dinner with John's parents to announce our happy news. Their reaction was, I must admit, a little disconcerting. Giving up a great career in banking to run a nonprofit for no salary is pretty much the opposite of the American Dream, so perhaps

I should not have been surprised that many people looked askance when we chose to be downwardly mobile.

"So…we've got some exciting news," John said over appetizers. "I'm leaving my job in January so Sarah and I can run the nonprofit together".

Pause. Silence. Long awkward silence. Count to thirty. The awkwardness grew more pronounced. I was the first to break the détente.

"So that's what we're doing," I added lamely but in a most chipper fashion. "And we're both really excited about it! So…. how's that goat cheese salad? Looks delicious! Can I try some? Mmmm. Really tasty. Don't you love goat cheese? The cranberries add a nice contrast, don't you think?"

After my skillful change of subject, nothing more was said that night about John's career change. Later, John's parents became some of our most steadfast supporters, which they remain to this day.

Over the years, many people have made well-meaning but irritating suggestions and thinly veiled criticisms about our life choices. Doing service work at the expense of your own financial security is not socially accepted, and it makes some people uncomfortable. "But what about your own children?" they would ask, in a mildly accusing tone.

I'm not saying everyone should make the same choices. I can say that the choices we've made have enriched us in ways we never expected. I've had to learn to live with the fact that not everyone approves of my choices and lifestyle.

In the final months of John's banking career, I was excited and a little afraid. It felt like we were about to jump off a cliff, with little tiny parachutes. We had already taken out a home equity loan to fund the charity. Now we would also have to sell the house, which didn't bother me, and cut back on vacations and eating out and many other treats, which did concern me a little. I like nice hotels, and sushi, and jeans that make my butt look good as much as the next person.

I also worried about how our new life direction would affect Maya and Luke, and their future opportunities. I saw my friends saving and sacrificing to give their kids every possible advantage in life – private schools, college funds, enrichments of every kind. Yet here we were going in the exact opposite direction. I believed that the decisions we were making would shape our kids' values in a positive way. That is the legacy I hoped to create for them, but sometimes I still had doubts and misgivings.

We knew it would take time for our organization to have enough income to provide any kind of salary. In the meantime, we would have to learn to live more simply, to subsist on what remained of our savings and on our love - for each other and for the survivors.

Despite my determination to support John's decision one hundred percent, things did not go smoothly at first. It was late January and bitterly cold when John joined the team. The team at that point consisted of me and three volunteers working from our basement. The four of us women were a merry crew, with female singer-songwriters always playing in the background, fragrant candles ever burning, and a girl-power vibe infusing all aspects of the workplace.

John totally destroyed the mood, barreling into our sanctuary with his brusque Wall Street manner, complete lack of diplomacy, and (I felt) a slightly know-it-all attitude. It was like having a marine band at a yoga retreat.

I was appalled and unable to hide it. For a while, nothing flowed easily. I felt sorry for the rest of the team because there was an awful lot of bickering that winter, and some outright shouting and even one or two especially heated arguments which we had to take outside.

For John's part, he felt unwelcome (by me, mostly) and unappreciated. I felt intruded upon, and forced into an awkward power struggle. It annoyed me that John did not see how ill-suited his working style was to this new context. For one thing, you can't tell volunteers what to do. You have to tactfully ask them, or agree together on tasks they will work on. You must be especially respectful and appreciative. For another thing, working with women is different than working with men, and working at a fledgling nonprofit is different from working at a high powered, fully staffed investment firm.

It took many months of growing pains before John and I figured out how to work together harmoniously, and we still occasionally butt heads. However, I have learned to appreciate John's attention to detail, his brutal honesty, and his analytic approach. For his part, John has adjusted his working style to become more diplomatic, and to appreciate the value of instinct. We've mostly learned to separate our emotions and relationship issues from business decisions.

I understand now why couples might actually choose to work together. To share a powerful dream, and to spend so much of your time and energy working together to achieve that dream is deeply bonding. Looking back, I can now see how our radically different natures actually made the organization stronger.

While I occasionally miss the breezy, uncomplicated times when John was a banker with a great salary, and I was writing music for soaps, there's no denying that the relationship we have today is far deeper and more meaningful.

To cope with the extra strain of that first year working together, I began trying to wake up a little earlier to have some personal and spiritual time to start the day. I found it tough to careen headlong into each day, cleaning, cooking, taking care of the kids, driving them hither and fro, and fighting slavery with empowerment and hope.

Sadly, it's been hard for me to maintain this sensible practice over the years. Like drinking more water and addressing my addiction to sugar, it is a practice I have to re-institute every three months or so. Will I ever grow my nails beyond stubs, lose that twenty pounds, eat slowly and mindfully, and maintain a daily meditation practice? At this point, it's looking unlikely, as long as so much of my energy is consumed with work. I'm choosing instead to focus on self-acceptance.

11 BACK IN THE TRENCHES, THIS TIME WITH FRIENDS

It could not be true that my father was dead.   But it was true.

In the middle of the second crazy, busy year running the charity, my brother called me early one morning. His voice didn't sound right and I knew before he told me that something was seriously wrong. Neill didn't mince words. "Dad has cancer, stage IV, colon".

No, this couldn't be right. I had seen my dad just two weeks ago. We had gone to a harvest fair and eaten cider donuts. He had been a little tired, that was all. I assumed he was just working too hard.

I couldn't believe this was happening again, only four years after losing my mom. My dad was sixty-four, and the loveliest guy you could ever wish to meet. He did not survive long with his cancer. The doctors told us he had a good chance for two or three years, maybe as many as five. He got three months.

I didn't have much time to grieve, because I had scheduled my first trip to India three weeks later, with three volunteers, my friends Alicia, Kim, and Bruce.

Our partnerships in Nepal, Cambodia and Thailand had grown closer over the past year. I felt it was time to visit India, the hub of human trafficking and child labor in South Asia. According to the latest Global Slavery Index, 18 million of the world's forty million slaves are in India. India is the place where most Nepali girls are taken. The fact that many girls are rehabilitated at Indian shelters, and that India's human rights movement was so long-established, was another reason I was keen to visit.

Ever since seeing 'The Day My God Died,' I had wanted to work with Sanlaap, the shelters featured in the film along with Maiti Nepal. Finally, I had made contact with someone at Sanlaap and had been invited to visit and explore the possibility of a partnership.

It had been a year since my last visit to Asia, and I was ready to learn more. Whenever I spend time with survivors, I get reenergized. Their courage and positivity is an antidote to the appalling case histories, to the cigarette burns on tender young skin, and even to the lesser struggle of long hours in front of a computer.

The four of us made a companionable travel party. Alicia has a wry, sarcastic humor and can-do attitude. Kim is the most easygoing person I have ever known. A potter by trade, she was entranced by the artistry of India and reminded us all to see its magnificence and not just its challenges. Bruce's practicality and wisdom provided a good balance to my fast and furious approach.

The four of us landed in Calcutta in the middle of the night. As soon as we de-planed, the warm night air and distinctive odor of Calcutta wafted over me. It was a medley of spices and wood fires with subtler notes of garbage and manure. I know it sounds like an unpleasant smell, but to me it was quite the opposite. Bizarrely, it felt like home.

Although I had never been to India before, that scent and everything else about it felt surprisingly familiar. Many elements of British culture still thrive in India, and that resonates with me, reminding me of my early childhood in England. Perhaps it felt familiar because this is where I was supposed to be, where my whole life had been leading, and so the scent of Calcutta gave me a sense of destination reached.

As I mused on this in a pleasantly jet-lagged fugue, I was brought back to earth by the arrival of our one-man welcoming party, the effervescent Chan, Program Manager at Sanlaap. With his unruly hair, skinny frame, Coke-bottle glasses and high energy, Chan bears an undeniable resemblance to Charlie Chan. He's a dynamo who has been fighting for the rights of vulnerable girls for over twenty years.

Driving through Calcutta to our hotel at 3:00 am was overwhelming and disheartening. This city of nineteen million has much to offer in terms of culture and history, but the poverty was like nothing I had ever seen. On every street and under every bridge, families made their homes from tarp or cardboard. The poverty was more extreme and on a much larger scale than I had witnessed in Nepal, Cambodia, or anywhere else.

Millions sleep on the streets each night. The pollution is intense, and because much of Calcutta dates back to the British colonial era, many of the buildings appeared to be literally crumbling into the ground. On first viewing, in the middle of the night, it felt almost apocalyptic. It was easy to see how desperate a parent could become in such circumstances, how vulnerable the little girls living on the streets were, in their tattered dresses and bare feet.

Chan took us to our hotel, which was in itself a wee bit disconcerting. It wasn't exactly dirty, but nor could you call it clean. The many young men who worked there were sleeping all along the narrow hallway, snoring peacefully. We had to step gingerly over their prone bodies as we made our way to our rooms. My room was quite dramatic, decorated in hot pink satin bedcover and curtains. I fell gratefully onto my thin, pink satin-bedecked mattress and was asleep in minutes.

The next day was Sunday so we had no meetings scheduled, and were able to visit some of the nicer parts of the city. At the Botanical Gardens, we saw what appeared to be a forest of Banyan trees, but was in fact one organism, the world's largest Banyan tree. The tree sends multiple trunks downward so it appears to be hundreds of trees, when in fact they are all connected. I knew this was a terrific metaphor for something, but I was too jet-lagged to figure out what.

We ate some extraordinarily good Tandoori food in the Muslim quarter. Calcutta has a large Muslim population, as well as Hindus (the majority religion) and a few Christians. On the whole, the groups coexist peacefully. However, the Muslim community is typically poorer, and many of the red light areas are in Muslim neighborhoods. When the staff saw that there were women in our party, they immediately whisked us into a back room and drew curtains around our table, shielding us from view of other diners. All the other diners were male. This was just one of the constant reminders that women in South Asia have a long way to go to achieve equality. Growing up in a culture with no equality and no public space for women ingrains in young girls the belief that oppression is a normal, acceptable way of life.

The next morning, we met up with Smarita, our contact at an agency called Apne Aap, a prevention program in the Kidderpore red light area. Apne Aap offered services to women trapped in prostitution and to their children. Many of the women in Calcutta red light areas were trafficked into prostitution as young girls. As adults they are no longer kept under lock and key, but they are stuck in this way of life because they see no other alternatives.

Calcutta has five major red light districts and Kidderpore is the poorest. Very young girls, who fetch a higher price, are exploited in the higher class areas.

Like many poor neighborhoods in Calcutta, Kidderpore is a warren of small alleyways, crumbling buildings and shanties with open sewage. Women and teenage girls sat listlessly on the sidewalk. We were instructed not to take photographs, as the women were sensitive about it, not wanting to be subjected to further shame or scrutiny.

At the end of a narrow alley we came upon the drop-in center, which was a complete contrast. Here were children learning to read and write, getting meals and a safe place to play. For the older girls, this was an alternative to being sexually exploited or trafficked alongside their mothers. Without education or jobs, the young teenage girls would be forced into prostitution. Over the course of the three years that Apne Aap had been in the neighborhood, the women of the community had come to trust the organization. It took that long to gain their trust because it was these women's first experience of kindness and respect.

Upstairs was the night shelter, where older girls can stay at night if they are not safe at home. Since most of the women in prostitution raise their children and entertain clients out of just one small room in a brothel, the situation is dangerous for their young daughters. If a client is bored or displeased with the mother, he can simply reach for her daughter.

Walking through the red light district in Calcutta for the first time was inexpressibly sad. At the same time, there was an abundance of compassion. Even in this place, where the darkest side of human nature is enacted night after night, people were fighting back. People were daring to hope.

After a long morning in the red light area, we met up with Chan to visit the Sanlaap shelter home. We drove out of Calcutta, past mile after mile of shantytowns and cardboard villages, arriving two hours later at the village where the shelter is located.

One hundred and thirty survivors, were living at the shelter. These girls had been trafficked and rescued by the police, by international rescue agencies, or by Sanlaap's own team. Most were barely into their teens. The youngest was ten. It is always painful to look at a young girl and know that she has been trafficked and sexually battered for months or years.

At Sanlaap, I learned more details about what life was like for these girls before they were rescued. In the brothels, the girls lived and served clients in tiny rooms just large enough for a single mattress. Most rooms do not have doors, but were separated by curtains. The girls slept during much of the day. When they awoke, they were given their one meal for the day. A few times a week they were allowed to shower. In the afternoon, they dressed and put on make-up in preparation for the arrival of customers. Some were sent out on the streets to entice men to come in. Others lined up in a hall or lobby so that customers could choose between fifteen or twenty girls.

Girls are forced to service ten or more customers a night in the brothel. They survive by detaching their minds and spirits from their bodies – complete disassociation. In rare cases, survivors are unable to reverse this defense mechanism. A few girls still trapped in this state wandered vaguely through the Sanlaap shelter, humming or crying or shouting, unable to connect or participate.

The job training program provided a welcome contrast to the sadness. Several girls were block-printing on twenty foot tables in one large room when we arrived. Block-printing is a traditional handicraft usually practiced only by men, yet these young women had become very skilled at it. They took hand-cut wooden blocks, dipped them in trays of paint, and repeatedly pressed or banged them down onto a large sheet of fabric, creating elaborate patterns. The girls gave us some of their old blocks to take home, as Kim wanted to incorporate the designs into her pottery. I chose some patterns and colors and placed an order for block-printed tablecloths.

The sewing room was equally lively, and the young women there were remarkably entrepreneurial. We chose a few samples to purchase, and thought we were all done, but the girls just kept bringing out more cool stuff for us to see, and of course we couldn't resist. Soon we had bought a huge pile of samples to carry home.

After rescue, girls generally live at the shelter for several years. Indian law requires that they stay at the shelter while awaiting the conclusion of their legal case before they can be sent home or live independently. This practice is controversial because it limits the freedom of victims. However, it does ensure that the girls are safe, and not re-trafficked in the vulnerable period following rescue. It also provides a strong community of peers and supportive adults to help the girls in their healing. Shelters are gated and protected by armed guards, because otherwise traffickers would soon snatch the girls back. Girls who recover in high quality shelters such as Sanlaap generally make a surprisingly strong recovery.

In the first few months after rescue, girls might also run away voluntarily, back to the brothels, because they have become so accustomed to that life of exploitation and have little hope that they could do anything else. Some have mothers or sisters back at the brothels. Most are so angry and upset that they can't make rational decisions. It takes months or years to rebuild a sense of self-worth.

We stayed at the shelter as night fell. We sang for the girls - 'You are My Sunshine' and 'My Favorite Things' in close harmony. They sang for us - Bollywood hits and Bengali folk songs. We drank tea and chatted and cheered them on as they danced and practiced judo.

"So can we look forward to a big order from you?" Chan asked hopefully. Of course I enthusiastically agreed. Our programs in India were officially underway.

I had no idea then how important that first trip to India would turn out to be. India has become the center of our operations, and Calcutta our headquarters. On that first trip, however, I was totally winging it. I was developing the program as I went along, while trying to appear assured and confident. I'm thankful for the open-mindedness of our early partners for trusting me and giving me the time and the guidance to figure things out.

The crowning point of that first day came later that night, when a girl anointed our foreheads with bright paint in preparation for the next day's Holi festival, the Hindu spring celebration of rebirth and renewal. After many hours in the car, the distress of the red light area, the raw pain of recently rescued survivors at the shelter, the heat and pollution and the slight but continual anxiety inherent in the situation, it was a rare moment of sacredness and peace.

12   BAND-AIDS AND ANT-RICE

"Take a good look at these people," instructed Vijay as we looked out at the crowd of a hundred women and children, some sick with AIDS and other serious illnesses. He spoke slowly, emphasizing every word, a tragic look upon his face. *"*Enjoy them, look at them deeply, because when you come back in one or two years, most likely they will no longer be with us".

Was it just me or was that a strange and slightly inappropriate thing to say? Thankfully no one in the crowd seemed to understand English. The four of us studiously avoided looking at one another. It was so macabre, and so bizarre, I was afraid we would burst into laughter, or tears, or both.

After a day off for the Holi festival, which involved being doused head to toe with brightly colored, semi-permanent paint, we had flown to Andhra Pradesh in Southern India. Our faces looked sallow and bruised from the Holi paint which would not wash off, no matter how hard we scrubbed.

The state of Andhra Pradesh has a severe trafficking problem, and other severe gender violence problems such as child marriage, but received little attention or funding to combat the problem. We were met off the plane by Vijay, the YMCA Executive Secretary for Andhra Pradesh.   Vijay's son and a friend (a former Bollywood film actor with a remarkable pompadour) completed the welcoming party. The three men carried enormous flower leis which they draped over each of us. I had never experienced such a VIP welcome.

With our new friends, we drove the four hours out to Kurnool, a provincial city of one million souls, which seemed to have only minimal services for the poor, trafficking victims, people with AIDS, or indeed anyone at all.

The drive was scenic, but it was the most terrifying drive I had ever experienced, as we were constantly passing giant tractors stacked high and wide with hay, missing oncoming cars by the tiniest of margins. There was no way our drivers could see around all that hay. It was a game of Russian Roulette every time we passed a hay truck. Of course the cars had no seat belts. I closed my eyes and prayed for a safe journey.

Kurnool is way off the beaten track– not in the wilderness sense because it is a busy, crowded city. It was just a different world in so many ways. It was short on infrastructure. We seemed to be the only Westerners, and people stared at us with surprised and curious expressions. Kurnool was extremely poor – and the poverty was driving the trafficking trade and the rise in HIV infection.

There were very few women out and about in the city. Even the lowest level jobs, such as cleaning hotel rooms, were held by men. We saw no women merchants, no women in the shops, cafes or restaurants, or in the hotel.

We spent a quiet evening on our hotel veranda, eating room service (*cue creepy organ music – this meal is not going to end well for some in our party*), and chatting.

The next morning, we visited Vijay's YMCA. His programs focused on AIDS prevention as well as trafficking. These issues, like many human rights issues, are integrally linked. Vijay was committed to attacking these problems, but his anti-trafficking program was only just getting underway.

After a quick walk-through, we saw the handicrafts that the women were making. The quality of the sewn and embroidered products was poor. I had a hard time imagining how we could sell them. Men from the community were making lacquered wood products. These were cool, but they weren't being made by women, or related to trafficking, so they weren't a good fit for our mission.

Next, it was time to meet the community, so we gathered under a tent with about a hundred women and children. Vijay ceremoniously introduced us in English and Telegu, the local language, expressing repeatedly his immense gratitude that someone had finally made it out to Kurnool.

That was when he made his odd and dramatic speech, encouraging us to appreciate this group of people while yet we could. We were asked to speak to the community members and offer words of encouragement. We handed out the Band-Aids and toys we had brought with us. People were really excited to receive these small gifts, but they seemed woefully inadequate. Band-Aids are not much help when you are living with AIDS.

Vijay had brought kilos of rice and oranges for everyone, so we helped hand those out as well. The rice was full of ants, which was no big deal to anyone there, but I found it a bit disheartening. People deserve better than charity rice full of ants, especially if they're struggling with HIV infection. However, I reminded myself, pity is useless and only makes people feel worse about their situation. We were in Kurnool to find a way to help, not to get morose.

We had planned to stay another night in Kurnool and then to drive five hours to a remote coastal area, struggling to recover from a recent tsunami, but Bruce and Alicia were beginning to feel really ill. They had contracted food poisoning, which in Alicia's case led to C-Dif, a serious bacterial infection which causes bowel bleeding and can even be fatal. Bruce and Alicia were worried about venturing even further from known civilization, and dreading the five-hour drive to the coast and eight-hour drive back to the airport the following day. With no bathrooms for that many hours, the drive would have been nightmarish.

We hated to let Vijay down, as he had put so much energy into our visit – the flower leis, the community meeting and the ant-rice, and did I forget to mention there were huge professionally hand-painted signs all over town announcing our visit? It was a difficult decision, but Bruce and Alicia were beginning to look terribly grim, so late that day, we began the drive back to Hyderabad.

The drive home was long and supremely uncomfortable for my sickly companions. There was not a single public bathroom, and scarcely a tree to squat behind. By the time we got to the city, Bruce and Alicia were doubled over with cramps. We urged the driver to hurry to the hotel. Unfortunately, when we finally arrived, the hotel we had booked turned out to be thoroughly unsuitable.

Bruce and Alicia went up to check out the rooms, hoping that they could use the bathroom while they were up there. Alicia was horrified when the clerk began masturbating (actually she used the more colorful term 'spanking the monkey') right in front of her. She tried to signal Bruce but he was doubled over in pain and distracted. "We can't stay here," she insisted.

Bruce was confused. The room looked nice enough to him, and he was unaware of the sex-offending clerk, but reluctantly, he followed Alicia back downstairs. Needless to say, after hearing about the clerk's obscene behavior, we unanimously decided to find another hotel. The next hotel was more expensive, but clean and seemingly sex-offender-free, so we decided to stay. There are some extravagances you simply should not do without.

An hour later, in the hotel bar, we reviewed the day's adventures. It had been a long and strange day, at times unsettling. The long drive, coupled with Bruce and Alicia's advancing illness, had been tense for everyone. Alicia recounted in further detail the unfortunate incident at the first hotel, and soon we were all doubled over, not with diarrhea but with laughter.

Walking into that hotel, I had felt discouraged, irritable and emotionally overwrought, but chatting and laughing with my friends soon restored me to sanity. I am thankful that I have never had to do this work alone. It would not have been possible to prevail without the support of wonderful friends like these, and many others along the way.

Bearing witness to other people's suffering is in its own way traumatizing. Of course, it is nothing like being the person who is actually suffering. The unbearable things that I see are a vivid reminder of how fortunate I am – not to be enslaved or to have my children trafficked, not to have AIDS, not to live under a tarp, to have clean water and health care, to be free and to have choices for earning a living. Perhaps most of all, I feel fortunate that I can take action against those things that I refuse to accept.

13   TEMPLE OF THE SUN

Despite going to bed with this mantra of gratitude, I awoke the next day with a monstrous stomachache. I thought I might have the same ailment as Bruce and Alicia, but it turned out to be just a stress-induced stomachache. The pain was a wake-up call for me. I like to pretend I'm unflappable - physically tough and emotionally well-armored.   My stomachache, which lasted for days, reminded me of my own limitations, my own (*gasp*) human frailty.

Bruce and Alicia flew home that afternoon as planned. Kim and I continued on alone to Orissa, a state in the northeast of India. We visited a potential partner which didn't pan out in the end because they didn't have the capacity to manage email communication. They took us to visit their schools for children who live on the railway tracks. The schools are right on the train platforms.

They also took us to visit the harshest red light area I have ever seen. The children there looked like ghosts.   Strangely, my camera malfunctioned that day and all my pictures came out semi-transparent, so the photographic record matches my memory. The children were just barely hanging on, flashes of light and life, transparent.

The red light school had been built on the only available plot of land in the red light area: a garbage dump. The smell was so appalling, it was difficult to concentrate on anything else.   Babies and toddlers were crawling through heaps of garbage, their mothers nowhere to be seen. Pre-teen girls hovered in the brothel doorways, their faces completely blank. That was one of the darkest places I have ever been.

The next day was Sunday and we had no shelters or red light areas to visit, which was a welcome relief, because I still wasn't well. Kim hired a car and driver for us to do some tourism and get out of our own heads.

Orissa is renowned for its ancient temples. Our first destination was the seven-hundred-year-old Temple of the Sun. Unbeknownst to us, this temple was built to celebrate fertility and sexuality in its many forms.

As we walked around the temple complex with a tour guide in the scorching heat, I began to find his commentary unnecessarily graphic. "See that wall carving there? That is a man and two women. And over there: two men. Here you see a woman with a dog". On and on he went, in the same manner. Fellatio, bestiality, orgies, phallic symbols of every shape and size, he described it all. *I can see it's a man with an ox!* I thought sullenly. I was in no mood for it, especially with my stomachache and being hot and sweaty, and feeling a bit sensitive after our visit to the world's harshest red light area.

Also I couldn't tell if this guy was just trying to shock us, the only Western tourists at the temple, or if this was his regular lecture. If it is, I couldn't imagine how it played with these conservative Indian families in their Sunday best. Kim didn't seem at all perturbed so I left her with our loquacious young guide and went to sit in the shade on the temple steps.

My peace and quiet was not destined to last, as I was immediately accosted by scores of Indian families wanting to have their picture taken with me. While the Temple of the Sun is a popular tourist site for Indians, it is infrequently visited by Westerners, and the surrounding villages where these families lived saw even fewer foreign visitors. I hope their holiday snaps were not totally ruined by the scowling lump that was me that day. I tried to muster a smile, but it came out more like a grimace.

Finally, Kim finished her tour. Leaning on her, I dragged my grumpy, stomach-crampy self back to the taxi. Back at the hotel, we were still not to find respite, as I was then harassed by an obese policeman in the lobby. He asked repeatedly for my home address and phone number, and urged me to write or call him, even after I explained I was married with two children. Corrupt police are a big problem in India, and in my weary state, I was feeling paranoid. *Could this guy get our key from the receptionist and attack me in my sleep?* I did not sleep well that night.

We flew home a few days later, grateful for our new partnerships, for all that we had been able to see and learn, and for our own blessed lives. I was grateful to eat something other than beans and thrilled to see my husband and children after two weeks away. I was fired up with more energy than ever to do something for the women and children I had met on my first trip to India.

14 DOWN TIME

Back home, my confidence in helping to solve Asia's human trafficking problem fizzled dramatically. I was just so...tired. I expected the usual jet lag, but it seemed worse than usual. Every afternoon around 3:00 I was compelled to go to bed. No matter how hard John lobbied me to 'STAY AWAKE UNTIL YOUR NORMAL BEDTIME!', there was no possible way I could do so. My ears began ringing, my head started to ache, my brain became foggy, and every cell in my body began screaming 'GO TO BED!!! GO TO BED RIGHT NOW'. So I did. Then at 3:00 a.m., those same cells would start screaming again 'WAKE UP!! Oh, sorry, did we wake you?'

In addition to the jet lag, there was something else, something suspiciously like depression. I realized my grief over the loss of my father had not just faded away. *'You can run, but you can't hide'* announced my grief, interrupting the brain cells screaming at me to go to bed. Grief will always find you. While I was traipsing around India, my grief was hibernating, patiently waiting for me to get home, where we could discuss our issues in private. With both my parents gone, I felt very alone. There was no one left to remember my childhood, no one to love me unconditionally. I was surprised by how untethered and out of balance I felt.

The next few months were difficult. I threw myself into my work, and tried to take joy in time with my family, but the loss of my parents continued to feel like a heavy burden. I learned to take comfort in the tiniest things —the sound of rain as I fell asleep, the flavor of a good meal, reading a funny book to my kids, every moment that I spent not in the hospital watching someone I loved dying. In the normal course of life, it is easy to take small pleasures for granted. The gift of death is that it makes you appreciate every single moment of life.

By late summer, I began to feel like myself again, and we had some exciting possibilities on the horizon. A large foundation had begun to fund anti-trafficking efforts, and they had reached out to us about the possibility of funding our work. Our meetings and phone calls with the foundation staff were very encouraging. One staff member told us she loved us so much she wanted to marry us! That certainly gave us confidence.

However, in August, we got the news that the foundation had rejected our proposal. My heart sank to the floor. Hadn't the staffer proposed marriage? Where went the love? More importantly, where went our grant?

John and I realized that we had badly miscalculated. We had planned on working one year without salaries, and had sufficient savings to do so. It was actually three years before we were able to draw any kind of salary. Tough times were a'coming.

I regretted that we had not cast a wider net by applying for grants from other foundations. Better late than never, I sent out a volley of letters seeking funding. Unfortunately, just like when I had applied for grants the year before, I received no positive responses or interest. I didn't yet have the right connections or expertise in writing grant proposals.

For the first time since jumping into this cause, I felt seriously insecure. Did I mention John could be overly blunt? "Well, I guess we'll just have to foreclose on the house and declare bankruptcy," he would say nonchalantly.

"What? No! We are not there yet!" I would reply in a panicked voice. We didn't know if we had enough money to make it to the next milestone, the point where product sales or donations could sustain the organization.

Let's face it, if your goal is to run a profitable business, you wouldn't hire traumatized survivors, nor would you manufacture products at shelter homes, where the power often goes out for hours a day, and where production is regularly shut down for monsoon rains, holidays, or social work crises. You would never choose a workforce which comes and goes according to their court cases, their trauma or other forces beyond anyone's control.

Not having time to wallow in disappointment, I resisted my fear and carried on. Thankfully, that Christmas, we had a breakthrough, which helped fund the following year's programs. Our work was featured in Family Circle magazine, in its holiday issue. It was only an eighth of a page, but the magazine has a circulation of millions, and the publicity brought in $40,000 in revenue, more than we had ever sold before. All of a sudden we were scrambling to fill all the orders. I was euphoric.

Every day of that holiday season was a madcap race to ship out products. Friends and volunteers came almost every day to help. The basement was piled high with bags and jewelry and boxes, and buzzing with energy and esprit de corps. The sudden increase in sales renewed my confidence that our idea could work. Despite the grief and disappointment which had dogged me earlier in the year, we ended it on a high note.

15 ROCK THIS CITY

The following month, we led our first volunteer trip to India. We brought twenty young Americans to volunteer for two weeks in a Calcutta red light district and rescue shelter. Most of the volunteers were rock band members, and friends of the bands, who wanted to learn about human trafficking so that they could raise awareness among their fans.

At times this trip felt ridiculously ambitious. Twenty people are a lot to manage in such a volatile environment. When we met the volunteers for the first time at Calcutta airport, they appeared dazed, confused, exhausted and very young. I am sure I looked equally shell-shocked (if not so young) when I landed in Kathmandu on my first Asia trip. Nonetheless, unlike me, each volunteer's hair was perfectly coiffed, artfully swept onto one side of his or her face. I still don't know how they maintained these spectacular hairstyles during a hot, humid two weeks in Calcutta, working at times right on the street.

While they knew salon secrets that I have yet to discover, some of the volunteers were quite naive about traveling in the developing world. There were at least twelve people in the group who had never been outside the U.S., and four guys from one band who had never ventured beyond the American South. At first the entire group clustered together as a herd. This drew a lot of unwanted attention in the streets of Calcutta, attracting beggars who spotted easy prey. As the trip went on, the volunteers became more comfortable and independent. I came to admire how they gathered each evening to 'share' – telling stories from the day and how their experiences affected them.

Bringing volunteers gave a different shape to my experience visiting the shelters. For the first time I had the chance to spend long hours working directly with survivors. On my earlier trips, I was learning, observing, making new connections and partnerships. Now I was engaging all day long with the girls, leading workshops, and building stronger and deeper relationships with our partners.

We sang until our voices were raw. We painted a mural and restored two rooms of a drop-in center in the red light district. We taught dance and cooking and English classes – anything we could think of to engage the kids. The younger children were always in my lap or holding my hands, the older girls at my side, just barely brushing shoulders. These are the moments I cherish the most, the memories I choose to recall in tougher times.

While the Indian staff members cared deeply for the kids, it was not their way to hug the children often, or hold them in their laps. They were busy holding everything together. We were blessed to have the time to indulge the children's need for one-on-one attention. I saw the healing power of love and affection as I had never seen it before.

On the first day, we took the team to the Apne Aap community center in the red light area. I led some drawing classes and helped the children to design a mural depicting their dream life. Even though they are growing up in an urban area, all of the children drew their dream lives in a village setting, with palm trees, thatched huts and elephants.

The children thrived that week with the attention and energy of the volunteers. They were growing up in such horrendous circumstances, living in one room of the brothel with their mothers. Worst of all, they have to see their mothers hurt and exploited night after night. There was an atmosphere of lawlessness and menace in the red light area, beginning every evening at around 4:00. The poverty was unbelievable. The children were underfed and many where neglected. They have to leave their home for hours every evening so that their mothers can work, and to avoid being molested by their mothers' clients.

The children also face tremendous stigma because they have been born into the red light area. It was difficult for them to attend local schools. They would be branded as red light children and ostracized. They rarely venture more than a few blocks from 'the lanes' of the red light district.

Nonetheless, the children were remarkable in their joyfulness and resilience. Pinky was one of the most exuberant. At six years old, she was still tiny, born to a woman who had been trafficked into prostitution as a teenager. Pinky's mother had late stage tuberculosis, but when she was not too sick, she still saw clients, having no other means to support herself and her child. Pinky was a born leader, so full of life it could barely be contained. All week long, she laughed and played with more enthusiasm than anyone. She sang the loudest and danced with danced with boundless energy and joy. She took up residence in my heart, along with many of the others.

With such a large group, and with an issue as sensitive as sex trafficking, things didn't always go smoothly *(Do they ever?!)* On Tuesday we took the volunteers out to the Sanlaap shelter. The plan was to offer the same art and music workshops we had been doing in Kidderpore. I failed to anticipate how different, and how much more difficult it would be to run the workshops in a shelter, where all the girls are trafficking survivors (as opposed to high risk children in a red light area) The median age of girls at the shelter was fifteen, compared to nine or ten at the community center.

Volunteering at the shelter was more challenging because of the obvious physical and emotional scars the girls there had. One girl was unable to walk because her spine was injured from being repeatedly raped at a young age. Another had lost an eye in a beating. Many girls had cigarette burn scars on their necks and hands. A small number were withdrawn and tearful, or angry and shouting, completely traumatized by their experiences. These girls were not ready to participate in arts workshops. Our volunteer group was also too large to manage in such a sensitive environment. After the first rather awkward day, we split into teams and sent small groups comprised of mostly women to Sanlaap.

Priya made a strong impression on me because of her unusual method of coping with her trauma, by singing. She had been rescued from a brothel at the age of thirteen. She had no contact with her family and did not know if they would ever be found. Many children like Priya, who were trafficked at a young age, cannot return home because they literally don't remember where it is. They have been traumatized by the trafficking experience and had little education prior to being trafficked.

They may not remember the name of their village or the larger towns near it. In some cases, they don't even remember their birth names. Priya spent long hours sitting with us and singing her favorite songs in a clear and beautiful voice. She told us she sings herself to sleep each night.

One of my favorite experiences from this trip was conducting product design sessions with the survivors at the shelter. It was encouraging to see the young women come to life in this situation, in which they were the ones with the expertise. The meetings were all about their ability, their creativity and problem-solving, not about their past abuse. Many people who interact with the survivors, like prosecutors, counselors, and journalists, have to focus on the trauma of their past. This is not a healthy place for survivors to remain long-term. The design sessions put the women in a different role: artists, experts, entepreneurs.

The experience strengthened my conviction that what the girls need most is not charity, but opportunity to build their own bright futures. The most important thing I can do for them is to keep creating more and better opportunities.

Chan, the Program Manager who I had met the previous year, said it best: "It only costs $500 of orders a month for five girls to support themselves independently," he told us. "Even the girls with AIDS…they might only have a few years to live, but they want to enjoy a little bit of normal life in that time. They want to leave something behind, something to show they were here on this earth".

Near the end of the second week, we ended up walking through the red light area at night. We left the drop-in center around 5:00 pm to walk to the night shelter. The drop-in center is located just outside the red light district, while the night shelter is right in the middle of it.

When we reached the lanes, it was early evening, and the women and girls were just beginning to hit the street. They lined up a dozen deep in alleys and behind doorways. Behind the brothel doorways were dark corridors with many doors to tiny rooms on either side. Girls clustered in the hallways, stalling for time, fixing their hair, or putting on lipstick.

Until that night we had all been compartmentalizing, keeping separate the joy we were sharing with the kids from our knowledge of their home lives. Having gotten to know and love many of the children, seeing the reality of their lives up close was disheartening.

I glanced at two teenage girls who stood by the curb, staring straight ahead. They wore heavy makeup and smiled at the men passing by, but their smiles didn't reach their eyes. They looked hollowed out, angry and hopeless. I could see that our presence shamed them, so I resolved to keep my head down and look straight ahead from then on. The last thing I wanted to do was make the women feel any worse about their circumstances.

I had made a major tactical area wearing flip flops that night, as a sewer channel ran directly through the narrow alley where we had to walk. I walked bow-legged to avoid it, but when others passed by in the opposite direction it was hard to avoid stepping directly into the sewage. And yes, there were rats, my personal fear factor. Knowing that the women and children have to spend every night in that place, I felt ashamed to dwell on my own discomfort or squeamishness. I bit the inside of my cheeks and marched on.

After five minutes that felt like thirty, we arrived at the night shelter. Inside the building, everything changed with the natural energy of children in a safe place. After visiting with the girls there, and seeing their home, we made our way back out of the red light area. It was getting later and the streets were now thronged with men. Some were alone, others in rowdy groups. Going to the red light area as an after-work recreational activity has sadly become a common practice. Running around and between the groups of men were little children. These were the children of the red light area, the very children we had come to know and cherish. The danger of the situation was obvious. Many of the men were drunk. Every man had come to the neighborhood to take advantage of vulnerable, desperate women.

The children have to play outside during working hours, because each family only has one room in the brothel. The menace of the streets is surely preferable to the pain of seeing your mother hurt and humiliated. These children's lives are full of impossible choices, a dangerous game they can never win.

John and I returned to our hotel shaken. We couldn't even find the words to comfort each other. After a few hours, I found my equilibrium, and this time it was my turn to bolster John. This was the first time he witnessed the grinding despair of a red light area.

I tossed and turned all that night, jerking awake at 3:00 am with a nightmare. I dreamed my kids were trapped in a bouncy house that deflated on top of them. They were suffocating as I tried desperately to get in to rescue them, but the primary-colored vinyl was impossibly heavy. No matter what I did, I couldn't get my children out.

This was a recurring dream, based on a real incident. Maya and Luke were playing in a bouncy house when it was punctured and began to deflate. I panicked briefly, but in the real life version, the house deflated extremely slowly and I was easily able to go in and walk my children out.

That night in Calcutta, it didn't take a team of psychoanalysts to figure out what the dream represented (*No matter what I did, I couldn't get the children out*). I was too agitated to fall back asleep, so I lay quietly until morning, trying to meditate, pray and relax myself into a calmer state of mind. I thought of my sisters still out on the streets, and made a silent promise to them.

I won't give up on you.

16 THE BEIGE COLONIAL - WHERE IT IS REVEALED THAT I AM NOT A NICE PERSON

I hate beige. I hate Colonial-style houses (the modern reproductions, not the actual historic homes). I read somewhere that 'beige is the oval of colors, and oval is the beige of shapes.' I would add that faux-Colonial is the beige and oval of house designs.

Given my strong views, it may seem odd that I found myself, at the beginning of this story, living in a beige Colonial-style home. Buying this house, that had so many elements I dislike, was one of those situations in life that somehow just got away from me. A week after we moved in, I remembered with a jolt that I hated beige and Colonial reproductions. Painting the house a brighter color would have helped, but that never happened because our lives took a different turn.

Shortly after we bought the house, I became involved in this work. A year later, as I mentioned earlier, John resigned to join me running the charity full-time. As soon as he decided to leave his job, we put the house on the market. The real estate market in New England was only just beginning its downward slide. We got an offer within a month, but it was contingent on the buyer selling their house. I was blithely confident this would happen and that we would be moving out right before John left his banking job.

I was wrong. That sale fell through and another six months went by with no offers. That was a busy and exciting time as we were building our programs and figuring out how not to kill each other. The hard part was that once a week we had to drop everything and clean the house for six hours so that prospective buyers could view it. We never did master the technique of maintaining a decent level of cleanliness to make clean-up for the showings less stressful.

In July, the first prospective buyers came back to us with a much lower offer. They had by now sold their house and were ready to move.

This second offer was still decent, and if I believed in regrets, which thankfully I don't, I would deeply regret not taking it. There was a lot of stress and strain yet to come, which could have been avoided, not to mention the hundred thousand dollars lost in the process.

At the time we were considering the second offer, we were confident that we were about to land a sizable grant. The grant would have been enough for us to being taking salaries, and along with our savings, would have been enough to keep up the payments on the house. We had taken out a home equity loan to fund the start-up of the charity. We were confident that our plan would pay off for the girls in Asia, and that we would soon be able to support ourselves, just more frugally than before.

My mother used to wake me every morning singing '*I beg your pardon, I never promised you a rose garden*'. She raised me with the understanding that life is both wonderful and hard. I was taught to be grateful when things are good, and never waste time saying 'life is unfair'. Struggle is one of the few things you can count on in this world.

With such an upbringing, I should have been prepared for the series of unfortunate events which followed. The housing market crashed. The market in our town, as in many other towns, was suddenly flooded with houses and bereft of buyers. Our monthly mortgage payment was huge because of the home equity line. The charity was not cash-flow positive and there was no way we could draw salaries.

A year passed, during which we cleaned and showed that house at least fifty more times. Our hopes steadily waned, my stress level rose, and foreclosure began to loom over our heads. I really did not want to take that route, especially since we had made choices that brought the situation upon ourselves. The responsibility weighed heavily.

Nearly a year after the second offer fell through, we finally got another offer. After little negotiation, we accepted it, and my joy and relief were truly monumental. We planned a big party and invited all our friends over to celebrate. We were literally dancing in the front yard when a double rainbow appeared directly over our house.

I am not proud of what happened next. A week after submitting their offer, the buyers inexplicably pulled out of the deal, claiming the width of the basement stairs were not up to code. *Were they serious?! The stairs were fine. I think they just changed their minds.*

Then, even though were hundreds of houses for sale in our town, they purchased a house just two doors down from us. *Ouch! What about my double rainbow? I had already thrown a party and danced in the yard. This could not be happening.*

All summer long, every time I saw these deal-breaking neighbors, I walked to the other side of the road and gave them the stink-eye. I fantasized about crashing my car into their hedges, their perfectly up-to-code staircases. I was livid, having come so close to a solution to my worries, and then watching it slip through my fingers.

How did the rest of that verse go that Freedom used to sing?

I beg your pardon, I never promised you a rose garden.

Along with the sunshine, there's got to be a little rain sometimes.

The rain lasted until late September, when finally someone bought the house, for real this time. Despite the bad karma I surely deserved for my unkind thoughts and dirty looks to our new neighbors, we finally sold our beige Colonial. By this time, it was a short sale, for $100,000 less than we owed. We were able to negotiate with the bank to share the loss, so it wasn't as bad as it might have been.

Best of all, the buyers were not ready to move into the house for another eighteen months, and agreed to let us rent back our house for a third of the going rate. This helped us tremendously as we worked to improve our credit, and pay off the debt we had steadily been amassing.

It was a miracle! I dug up the St. Joseph statue I had buried upside-down in the yard and doused him with champagne. I walked around in a state of euphoria for weeks. We no longer had the looming anxiety of foreclosure or an enormous monthly mortgage bill to pay, and we didn't have to worry about moving for another year and a half.

While I had reason to be disgruntled when the house sale fell through, I'm not proud of how I behaved that year, especially to the neighbors who almost bought our house. I don't want anyone to read this book and think, '*Wow, Sarah is such a nice person. I could never do something like that because I am not as nice as her*'.

I asked a few of my closest friends for an honest assessment of my niceness or lack thereof. "No, you really aren't that nice," one friend responded. "I mean you are a loving friend, but you aren't one of those really sweet-natured, selfless people. You can be pretty rigid and opinionated actually". Another agreed: "You definitely don't have to worry about being *too* nice. You can be quite bossy and judgmental at times. But we love you just the way you are!" John concurred. It was unanimous.

So there you have it. I am thought by those who know me best to be (at times) rigid, opinionated, bossy and judgmental. I admit I do love judging. It's so satisfying! I also love doing things my way, which I truly believe is the best way...

This is hardly an exhaustive list of my flaws. I promise I have many more. And that's okay! You don't have to be super-nice or super-anything to change the equation for people in need. You just have to be willing.

And relentless.

Loving.

And very patient.

17 WHY DID YOU NOT COME SOONER?

A few years into this journey, I came to realize that a good deal of the work required to make our program succeed was repetitive and tedious. Rather than spending my days counseling survivors or conducting rescue raids, as I had once imagined, I was spending my days putting products in bags and putting the bags in boxes and sending the boxes to customers. I also spent eight-ten hours a day in front of the computer, often doing mundane tasks. Like anyone running their own business or nonprofit, my workday never really ended. There was always more that needed to be done urgently and no one else willing or available to do it at 10:00 on a Friday night. While the tasks I do change, that is still the situation today.

That fall, we rented a storefront to sell survivor-made products and raise awareness in our community. That was not one of our grand successes. We were neither gifted nor committed shopkeepers. The first few weeks were fun enough. Maya and Luke, then seven and eight, loved working the cash register. Volunteers came, bringing their own kids, and it was a nice way to spend time with my kids while working. Spoiler alert: that is the last good thing I have to say about running the shop.

On the not-so-fun side, there was the fact that the storefront, a tiny building which must once have been a small barn (for miniature horses perhaps?) or shed, was not designed to have two floors. The ground floor consisted of one small room of normal height, while the staircase and upper floor had ceilings only five feet high. I was constantly banging my head on the way up the stairs. If we needed to work upstairs, we had to crouch or crab-walk. Of course, I would get distracted and hit my head up there too.

Our small team dividing its time between staffing the store and running all the other aspects of our organization. This included overseeing our programs in Asia, working with partner agencies, managing the online store, ordering products, packaging and shipping orders, fundraising, dealing with survivors' needs and crises, and so on. When a customer came through our doors, it often felt more like an unwelcome distraction than a great opportunity.

When our customers were kind and supportive – as most were – I would quickly get over my frustration and would enjoy the time spent serving them. When they were annoying –so horrified by the cause that they scurried backwards out of the shop, or bargaining over prices as if this were a flea market – it was irritating in the extreme. There were times when the workload seemed overwhelming, endless, and downright tedious. For all such moments, this story has become my touchstone.

I heard it from a real-life superhero, Kailash Sidyartha, who later won the Nobel Peace Prize. Kailash and his organization, BBA, have rescued over 60,000 men, women and children from slavery and child labor in India over the past two decades. They have rescued many from carpet loom factories, a brutal industry in which 300,000 Indian children are entrapped. That number used to be 600,000 before Kailash and other activists began to break the stranglehold of the traffickers.

Children in these workshops often do not see the light of day for months or years. Their small fingers are prized for making the tiny, elaborate knots of Oriental rugs. Traffickers promise their parents that the children will be educated, will work part-time, and will be able to send money home. Many of these parents never see their children again. Children work from morning to night, and those that fail to please their masters sleep chained to their looms. It's Dickensian times again in the carpet factories, and many do not survive it.

On one occasion, Kailash told me, he rescued thirty women and children from a carpet factory. All were being taken to BBA's shelter for emergency care. The children stay at the shelter for six months to a year, receiving remedial education and nutrition. Many have been so malnourished in the looms that they grow six inches or a foot in a year once they are properly fed. Many have facial scars that look like acne scarring, because of the poor ventilation and low air quality in the carpet factories, and also because of the stress on a five or eight-year-old child who is removed from his family and made to work twelve hours a day.

Raids are conducted by rescue organizations, sometimes with local trusted police, but in other cases by unarmed citizens. Before raiding the factory, investigators stake out the premises to see who is coming and going. They interview local people and follow leads from relatives or neighbors. Many activists have been hurt, killed, or wrongfully arrested in such raids, because human trafficking is a form of organized crime, and the slaveholders are prepared to defend their livelihood. Police are often bribed to overlook child labor and slavery. They too are motivated to protect their source of income, even if it means arresting innocent people. The raid usually involves a heated confrontation with lots of shouting, threats or physical violence.

After this particular raid, seven rescued children were riding in Kailash's car. He had fruit on hand for them, including bananas, which must be the most common fruit in India. Even in the most remote villages, bananas are universally available. Asha, who was about eleven, picked up one of the bananas and took a bite without peeling it. "What kind of potato is this?!" she asked, sputtering.

Asha, who had worked in the factory with her family since early childhood, did not recognize food other than rice and potatoes. She could not remember ever seeing a banana. This is what slavery does to children. They are completely isolated and lack basic knowledge.

After receiving an explanation and help peeling the fruit, Asha and the other children devoured the bananas with the greatest pleasure. A few silent minutes passed. Then Asha spoke up again.

"Why did you not come sooner?" she asked matter-of-factly. At first Kailash laughed. He thought she meant 'Why did you not come sooner, because these bananas are so good!"

He was appalled when she continued, "Why did you not come sooner, before my little brother died?"

'Why did you not come sooner, before my mother was raped in front of everybody?"

"Why did you not come sooner, before my childhood was over?"

Kailash, who has rescued thousands, was saddened and shamed by this child's words. He vowed to redouble his efforts until every child slave in India has been freed.

Whenever I experience a moment of doubt, self-pity, fear or boredom (like when doing my year-end accounting), I think of Asha and Kailash, and renew my commitment. I know that in some small way, everything I do for our survivors helps move them closer to freedom and independence. In an age where instant gratification is our normal, it's hard to wait for anything. Ending or even drastically reducing trafficking and gender violence is a marathon, not a sprint. Each product sold, each woman trained and employed, each child educated, every dollar raised to build a shelter or feed the girls living there is one step closer to getting the job done.

Many children like Asha, in child labor or slavery - are hoping against hope that someone will come and rescue them. Many girls have told me that even when they finally accepted their fate, there was a tiny piece of them that still imagined that their mother or father, or a kind stranger would come and pull them to safety. As long as there are children in slavery hoping for rescue, I need to keep doing everything I can to answer their cries for help, even when it's hard, even when it's boring, even when I feel hopeless or ineffective.

We who believe in Freedom can not rest until it comes

-   Sweet Honey in the Rock

18 THE MOTHERS

Before I knew it, I was back in Calcutta, nearly five years since my first viewing of 'The Day My God Died'. Having learned some important lessons on our first volunteer trip the winter before, this time I brought a much smaller group of ten people who I knew well, and who had already been involved with our organization for a while. Despite this good planning, things got off to a rough start.

John was supposed to lead the trip with me, but he broke his leg the day before we were due to leave. As we had ten people counting on us, I had to leave him in the care of his parents and lead the group by myself.

Our team got off the plane at 6:00 am after a thirty-hour odyssey. We were tired to the bone. I for one have always needed my beauty rest, so I was a little short on tolerance and compassion, which proved to be a major occupational hazard.   (Remember when I revealed that I'm not always a nice person?)

We checked into our hotel, a simple but functional establishment in the tourist district. *Note to self: Do NOT stay in the tourist district!* The room I shared with my friend Dan was right next to a disco, which played loud and appalling Hindi disco music until 2:00 a.m. each and every night. Even with our limited knowledge of Indian pop music, we could tell this was terrible music. At 2:00 it would stop at last, only to be replaced by a chorus of jackhammers which continued until dawn! Thankfully we brought a good supply of Advil PM without which we would not have been able to function.

Our flight had landed early in the morning, and I had hoped that we would have time to take showers and freshen up before starting our first day of work in the red light district.

Woman plans, God laughs.

Instead of resting and showering, I spent what little time I had in an argument with my friend John McDonagh. McDonagh was a little freaked out by Calcutta in general and our hotel in particular. To be fair, the hotel must have looked rough around the edges to someone unfamiliar with Calcutta, what with the guys sleeping in the hallways, the tiny, stained bathrooms, the lack of working locks on the doors, and the creepy Santa Claus figure in the lobby. It was a combination of the Santa we know and love, and a Hindu temple sculpture, scowling and underweight – an unappealing hybrid.

McDonagh and I worked out our differences eventually, after some yelling and stomping around on his part, and some silent fuming on mine. Silent fuming is a recurring theme for me, but hey, nobody's perfect. I'm working on it. McDonagh went on to become one of our most loyal and effective volunteers. His passion is what made him such a valuable member of the team. It also made him, at times, a hothead and a pain in the hindquarters.

Unfortunately, our argument that morning left no time for anything else, so we each put on a happy face, and headed to the shelter. Entering the red light drop-in center from the chaotic streets of Calcutta was like walking into an oasis of serenity and joy. We all breathed a sigh of relief, and our earlier tensions evaporated.

Our first activity was a women's rights and legal rights workshop with women in prostitution and their teen daughters, as one of our team members was a lawyer. The women had mostly been trafficked into prostitution as young girls, from rural villages in India, or from Nepal or Bangladesh. They were brought first to the high-end brothels in other red light areas of the city, where the youngest, prettiest girls fetch the best price.

As time passed, and their street value decreased due to age or illness, they were no longer valuable to their traffickers and drifted to Kidderpore – the poorest of the red light areas - with their children. In the brothels of Kidderpore, frequented by local workingmen, the mothers are forced to engage in more violent and dangerous sexual activities in order to attract clients. They are no longer valued for youth or beauty. Desperation is their only asset.

I was humbled by their courage and stoicism. In their situation, I would be tempted to put my face down on the sidewalk and give up. Somehow these women keep going. They have children to care for, vulnerable daughters and sons. The most heroic of the mothers show up at the drop-in center, fighting for a way out for their kids.

"It's too late for us," they say. "Just do something for our children". Of course, we don't think it's too late, and neither do the local groups working in the red light areas. This center and others like it exist to offer the possibility of a different life to these mothers *and* their children.

I could only compare myself to these women in one shared experience, and that was as a mother that would do anything to protect and provide for her children.

During the workshop, we discussed legal rights in the US and in India, comparing notes on each country's suffrage and human rights movements. The Indian women and girls were astonished to hear that American women also suffer family violence and rape. They imagined our lives here to be like a Hollywood movie – sheltered by virtue of our wealth and white skin. They were intrigued, and found solidarity in the fact that women in the western world have also had to struggle for their rights.

By 4:00 p.m., in the weak winter light, it was beginning to get dark. Suddenly, in the middle of the workshop, the mothers rose as one, and without a word, left the building. Those of us who remained fell silent. My team looked at me questioningly, but they already knew the answer. They were just hoping for a different answer. The women had to leave the human rights workshop to go back to the streets for another night of exploitation and violence.

It was becoming clear to me that providing economic alternatives wouldn't be enough. We would need to also provide education and advocacy to protect the rights of women like these, to give them the tools to defend their own rights.

The girls at the drop-in center became restless after their mothers left. Someone proposed a song, so we sang it, then another and another. We held hands and sang together, in English, Hindi and Bengali, until the darkness fell around us completely.

19 PIVOT

The next day, we painted the night shelter a jaunty blue. Later in the week, we painted a mural with the kids from the red light district. Painting was a bit of a challenge, because the 'latex' paint we had purchased turned out in fact to be oil paint. We had to get very creative with supplies and clean-up was a serious challenge (less said the better).

We've painted a lot of murals over the years, in red light areas and rescue shelters and later in our own offices and centers. I am passionate about the healing power of the arts. I first learned about the power of artistic self-expression for traumatized kids in my twenties, when I worked at Creative Arts Workshops, an agency serving homeless children in New York City. My boss and mentor, the artist Brookie Maxwell, pioneered an approach for healing through the arts that has had a huge influence on my work with survivors.

Brookie taught me that traumatized kids do not always want or need to talk about what is bothering them. Sometimes they are so upset by the problems in their life, they become unable to function and shut down completely. It's a vicious cycle, because then nothing in their life is working and they aren't achieving anything. Their self-esteem spirals downward.

When traumatized children have the chance to refocus their attention on a challenging art project, they can soothe themselves. Then they may become ready to talk constructively about their problems. When they succeed in creating something beautiful, the satisfaction of that achievement gives a boost to their self-esteem.

"I understand you are upset about having to go into foster care," Brookie would say to a distressed child, "and we can certainly talk about that later. But right now, we're building this Spirit Box" (or painting this mural, or constructing this giant metal sculpture).

Working with trafficking survivors, I've learned that when a person's pain has come through the body, as in the case of sexual or physical violence, it can't just be talked out. Some of the pain has to be released through the body, because the pain has come through the body, and often it is still held there. Dance is a powerful tool for healing, and so is painting murals, because it is physical, and requires planning, concentration and team effort. The survivors get to see and feel pride in their accomplishment every time they walk past the mural. This is one way we can leave a piece of our love behind for them.

When I wasn't painting with the kids, I careened around Calcutta, to a series of meetings with local partner organizations. Our projects were growing and evolving. Whereas in my early visits to Asia, I was meeting potential partners, learning and exploring, now we were deepening our relationship with partners, and had a clear strategy for growth.

In the first few years of our project, we partnered with shelter homes to create jobs for survivors. The jobs were located inside the shelters, and managed by the shelter staff. Sometimes we helped our shelter partners to launch new training programs, which we supported with donations and business consulting. This approach made use of the experience of people already working on the front lines. I didn't feel it was appropriate to come barreling in telling people what they should do to end trafficking in their own communities. I believed we should start by supporting the good efforts that were already in place.

After a few years, however, we reached the limit for how much we could accomplish at shelter-based programs. For one thing, the shelter staff were dealing with so many urgent crises all the time, they usually couldn't make employment a priority. Their expertise was in social work, not business. Sometimes it was difficult to convince them to make changes to improve the quality of products or increase productivity.

An even more serious problem was that the jobs programs inside the shelter homes often didn't provide enough income to enable survivors to rejoin society and support themselves independently. Women who were ready to move out on their own needed jobs in the outside world. They wanted jobs that were not associated in any way with the stigma of trafficking and prostitution.

It is vital to listen to the people you are trying to serve. We are committed to vigorous self-assessment, to regularly asking our survivors what they want and need, and asking ourselves whether our program is meeting their needs in the best possible way. If there are ways in which it isn't, we adjust, and change direction if necessary.

We had been supporting jobs programs in shelters for several years when we realized that this system wasn't meeting all of our goals. We had to find another way. It was time to pivot. We've had to go through this cycle many times. It made me uncomfortable at first. It required admitting that some things weren't working. To put it another way, it meant admitting some things were failing.

Several times when we've realized that things weren't optimal, we had to completely rethink and reorganize the way we worked. This was always difficult, but I've never regretted doing it. Every time we've looked at our work, decided it could be done better, and made changes, our program got better at serving survivors.

In this case, we decided it was time for us to launch an independent employment center in India, outside of the shelter system. Our friends at the Sanlaap shelter liked the idea, and agreed to send some of their survivors to live and work at our new center. Sanlaap's founder, Indrani Sinha, told us that the new center could help solve one of her biggest problems. Older girls who could never return home were taking up room at her shelter for years, even after they had reached adulthood and no longer needed shelter services. She needed the space for newly rescued girls.

At that point, we had our first staff member in India. This was Becky Bavinger, who was just twenty-three years old at that time. Becky had wisdom beyond her years and a natural rapport with survivors, many of whom were around the same age. Smarita Sengupta joined our team that winter also. Smarita's gifts as a counselor and her relationships in Calcutta proved to be hugely valuable.

Together with our friends at Sanlaap, we launched a new employment center outside of the shelter. To prepare the survivors for managing their own businesses one day, we offered workshops in business and English. We soon saw that the girls loved learning about business. Their thirst for knowledge in any subject is intense. Many of them had been forced to leave school at a young age, while their brothers were able to continue studying.

Sharmila, one of the first survivors to work at the new center, told us how the work became part of her recovery. "At first you just join in the vocational training for something to do", she said. 'Then you start to think maybe you could make a living out of it. It gives you a sense of self-worth for the first time. Many girls think at first they are just going to be sold again by the people at the shelter. They want to run away and go back to their village and family. That wouldn't be safe because many of us were sold by our family, or neighbors... But after a period of weeks, months, or years, you start to believe that you really could have another kind of life".

20 WRITTEN ON MY BODY

All too soon, it was time to go home. On the final day, as always, I found it almost impossible to say goodbye to the children. These were the kids with whom we had sung lullabies while their mothers left to walk the streets. These were the kids who walked us through the red light area at the end of each day, shielding us from menacing groups of clients. How do you walk away from that, leaving them in a place which is so dangerous?

We hugged each other tightly, and the girls drew intricate henna designs on our hands as a parting gift. I liked the henna because it gave me a visual reminder of the children for the next few weeks. I gathered the children together and made them a promise: "We love you. We will keep coming back. And while we are away, we will be working every day for you".

I had become especially close to one of the girls, Hansa. She was thirteen, scrappy, bossy and radiant. She was a modern-day Little Orphan Annie (not the red hair and freckles, but the feisty leadership and refusal to back down). Hansa had no trouble subduing a group of fifty boisterous children, herding them into an orderly line so we could hand out paintbrushes or snacks.

Hansa became my right-hand woman, always at my side with a helpful translation or crowd control. She anticipated my needs, for a cup of tea, or a moment of rest in the shade, just like any loving daughter. I fantasized about adopting Hansa, but she already had a mother. Her mom was one of the women who had to leave the workshop on our first day to walk the streets.

A year later, Hansa would be working the streets herself. She was a girl I was not yet able to help, a loss it still hurts to recount. Of course, I did not know this yet, as she sat with her head buried in my shoulder that last day, her love - like the henna - written on my body.

I got to know dozens of remarkable women and children on that trip. I met women who had overcome the oppression and were learning to trust. I met mothers who were rising above their own pain to fight for their children.

Mira was the most remarkable of all. She worked for Apne Aap as a community organizer. Prior to that, she had been trafficked and exploited for decades. Unlike other women her age in the community, Mira looked healthy and robust for her forty-plus years. Her roundish build and soft features suggested South Pacific more than South Asian heritage. Mira had a raucous laugh which could be heard echoing through the halls. She was effusive in her love and appreciation for our team. She showed her affection by shoving handfuls of food directly into our mouths. Given the lack of running water in all the homes in the district, it might not have been the best idea to have her hands in our mouths, but it was such a loving gesture, we couldn't refuse.

Mira's son Rakesh was one of the children participating in our workshops those two weeks. He came without fail every day after school and worked until it was dark and we had to put the paints away. Then he helped us clean the brushes.

At the end of our first week, Mira told us her incredible life story. She had been trafficked as a young girl from Bangladesh. She became pregnant and gave birth to a daughter. When her daughter was thirteen or fourteen, Mira's pimp/'husband' trafficked her child. The girl was sold off to the Middle East (Mira thinks but is not sure) and was never seen again.

Some years later, a local agency came into the community offering support and opportunities for people to come out of the sex trade. Mira, then in her early forties, was past the prime age for prostitution, so she was no longer a captive. The bars and chains that kept her enslaved were poverty and stigma.

Mira took the opportunity that was offered and left the sex trade, becoming a community advocate. Incredibly, the husband who had been her pimp made the same choice. He chose to stop exploiting women and girls, and instead to help them by working as a security guard and handyman at the red light drop in center.

In an act of mercy and generosity which I cannot begin to comprehend, Mira forgave her husband for the years of abuse, and for selling her daughter. Together they were raising a son, who was not their biological child. They took him in after his mother died or ran away.

All the trivial little things I had ever wasted my time worrying about were thrown into perspective, in the face of this monumental compassion and forgiveness. Mira's daughter may be gone forever, but her son will have a bright future because Mira took his life in her hands and refused to let go. She found the strength to rise above the violence and loss of her past and to focus on building a future for herself and her adopted son.

Forgiveness truly is a divine act. Taking hold of a child in need and refusing to let go is equally divine. What incredible things could we all do if we followed Mira's example?

21 BLOOD

Three months later, I was back in Asia with Alicia. We planned to spend a few days in Calcutta at our new employment center, then travel to Nepal to meet a new partner agency. Perhaps I should have known this trip would not go smoothly, when we spent twelve hours at Boston airport, waiting for a snowstorm to subside, before being given a hotel room for the night and finally shipping out the following morning.

Our lives had gotten so hectic by that point, twelve hours in the airport felt kind of like a spa day. Okay, there were no massages, no harp music, but we did have cocktails, we ate three meals in a restaurant, we slept in a nice hotel, and we had the luxury of time to chat and to pore over magazines. If you think it is lame to count twelve hours at Logan Airport as a spa day, then all I can say is you have never been a working mom.

We finally made it to Calcutta, a day later than expected. Unfortunately, my luggage did not make the cut. I usually pack all the essentials in a carry-on bag in case this happens, but had not done so this time.

I was not to be reunited with my suitcase until we flew out of Calcutta airport two weeks later, so I had to get creative with fashion. Indian women tend to be petite, and the clothes sold off the rack in Calcutta were out of the question for my corn-fed American proportions. There were a few tourist shops selling cotton clothes to backpackers. I found two very special pairs of trousers that fit my generous behind. One was a baggy, drop-crotch number that looked like a giant canvas diaper. The other was rather like a long loincloth over fitted pants. Did I mention it was purple with gold lace trim at the ankles? *Jaunty.*

Finding shoes to fit was out of the question, as our time was extremely limited, so for the first few days I had to make do with the hiking boots that I was wearing on the airplane, plus one black skirt, and thankfully a toothbrush.

Of course (since remember I already said things weren't going smoothly on this trip?) I got my period on my first night in Calcutta. Not having my luggage meant I didn't have the usual necessities, so we stopped and picked up some feminine products, but they weren't the ones I was used to, and that led to problems later. Also, I only had one pair of underwear which I had to wash out every night along with my loincloth and diaper trousers.

We arrived late to Calcutta on the first night and our first meeting was early the next morning. This meeting was with two Indian doctors who ran a hospital called Calcutta Mercy, which provides excellent care to rich and poor alike. The two men were developing a new program to provide health care to women and children in red light areas, and we were meeting with them to talk about getting medical care for the women and children in our programs.

They chose the venue and it was the Taj hotel, which is seriously out of our league. We usually just conduct our meetings on the dusty floor of a shelter home. If it's an important meeting, we might get folding chairs, but that's about as fancy as it usually gets.

The doctors looked mildly surprised at my strange attire (purple loincloth and hiking boots) but politely declined to comment. It was a productive meeting and we were all excited about the possibilities for collaboration. Ultimately we were able to bring thirty kids from the red light area to their hospital for checkups as a result of this meeting.

As the meeting was winding down, I came to the horrifying realization that blood was leaking through my clothes onto the fancy chair of this oh-so-fancy hotel. *Oh no!* Since the meeting was almost over, I excused myself to go to the bathroom, assuming the others would also get up to leave and maybe no one would notice the blood stain on my chair. Deftly, I stood up and in one fluid movement pushed my chair under the table. Then I delicately backed away and twirled around the corner towards the Ladies' Room. Alicia came with me, but the doctors stayed at the table, deep in conversation.

In the bathroom, I was able to manage the situation and fortuitously, the loincloth served to cover any stains on my trousers. Immensely relieved, I returned to the restaurant so we could say our goodbyes and beat a hasty retreat. With any luck the others would already have left the table and would be waiting in the lobby.

Imagine my dismay when instead of leaving the table, one of the doctors had actually slid over into my chair to converse with this colleague! I was torn between suicidal mortification and hysterical laughter, and ended up choosing the laughter. I prayed really hard that he would not get a stain on his trousers and thankfully my prayers in this regard were answered.

Sometimes I feel like a whirling dervish, hurtling through life, barely in control. My kitchen is a mess, and I'm forever losing my wallet or leaving bloodstains on the chairs of posh hotels. But what can you do? The day was only just beginning, so after offering a year's worth of hilarity to my friends, I hitched up my loincloth and got on with my day.

22   UNBEARABLE

"This is <u>not</u> a shelter, children's home or welfare program. It is our family. Please behave accordingly".

So read the hand-painted sign in the entryway of Apple of God's Eye, the first organization - or rather the first family - that we met with in Kathmandu. This team is lovingly raising 250 survivors, high risk children, and former street children in five family home settings.

The story of how this group got started is one of the grimmest I have ever heard. Twelve years earlier, Brazilian pastor Dr. Jose Rodrigues was walking through Kamathipura red light area in Mumbai. Kamathipura is the world's largest red light area with a captive population of over 200,000.

Dr. Rodrigues was shocked to see a dead Nepali girl of about twelve lying on the sidewalk. Her body was naked and wrapped in a thin sheet. To his horror, a garbage truck then drove up, and some men threw the child's body into the truck. Dr. Rodrigues was appalled, and uncomprehending. 'She's just a Nepali whore,' onlookers explained with a shrug.

When I first heard this story, I felt physically ill. I can't imagine how Dr. Rodrigues felt seeing the scene with his own eyes. It would have been perfectly natural for him to turn away in horror, or throw up his hands in helplessness. Instead, he chose to take action to prevent this atrocity from happening to other girls.

Dr. Rodrigues decided to attack the problem at its source - in Nepal. He gathered support from the Brazilian Evangelical community to send Silvio and Rose Silva to Nepal. Silvio and Rose brought their own young son, and soon found themselves parenting twenty more children in their own small apartment. Over the next 16 years, their family grew. Today they oversee six homes, a school for 200 children, a sustainable farm and eco-lodge, and more. The girls who first came to live in their home are now leaders and managers of the projects.

I've visited many shelter homes over the years. I've often been impressed by pleasant surroundings and a good atmosphere, but this truly was a whole new world. The level of recovery was so high, you would never guess these girls came from such difficult backgrounds. Each child was squeaky-clean, well-educated, fussed over, deeply known, and greatly loved. They were affectionate and confident. The older ones communicated with ease in Nepali, Portuguese and English, as well as their own tribal languages   Somehow these kids just didn't look like shelter home kids. They looked much more like my own kids. They looked like they belonged to someone.

Some of the teenage girls performed a song they had written about their experiences. The song was terribly poignant but also hopeful. One girl played the guitar while fifteen others sang the tune. The girls had recently won a city-wide competition for their singing and songwriting.

One team of young women, led by the indomitable Mamata Tamang, was in charge of repatriation of Nepali survivors from India. They travel often to India, fill out endless paperwork, negotiate with frustratingly bureaucratic government agencies, fight to get girls repatriated, and accompany rescued girls back to Nepal. Later, these young women got legal training so they could argue cases in lower courts in Nepal.

Some survivors had trained as dental hygienists and took charge of dental cleaning for the younger kids. Others were house-parents in the homes. Everyone was doing her part. The girls and boys who grew up at Apple are able to take on these leadership roles because they have received an excellent education, and because the Apple of God's Eyes team has nurtured their potential.

I felt the love of that place deep in my heart. Each child, upon arrival, is given a bed with pretty patterned sheets and is taken to the store to pick out any stuffed animal or doll they desire. Many have giant stuffed bears on their beds. Silvio gives them the bears to show them that they are free to be children again.

For trafficking survivors, bedtime has been a time of fear and violence. For them to have their own bed and to be safe in it is transformational. This is how children are supposed to be living, not locked up in tiny rooms being used by callous men, not sleeping alone and endangered on the streets.

Silvio and Rose were committed to maintaining the family-style ambience at any cost. Silvio had recently had to turn down a large grant from the United Nations because it stipulated that he would have to hire a full time driver and security guard. "Do you have a security guard and driver for your family?" he asked me. Of course I do not. Silvio knew that adding those things would turn his home into an institution. He and Rose believe in keeping it simple. As the sign said, this is a family.

This was a beautiful lesson in the value of sticking to your vision regardless of the carrot dangled in front of you. Silvio and Rose could have doubled their project size with that grant, but it wouldn't have been the same at all. It would have been bigger, but less special. It would have been less in tune with the needs of the children.

I thought many times that day, and in the days to follow, of that poor dead child wrapped in a sheet on a Mumbai pavement. As long as Silvio and Rose, and I, and all of us, do not forget her, as long as we are motivated by her story to do something for others in need, her life and death will not be in vain.

We can all refuse to bear the unbearable. We can all do something to change the equation.

23   A TINY STORE AND A LARGE BOAR

Next we were off on a hair-raising six hour drive to Hetauda, a smaller city in the mountains of rural Nepal, near the border with India.   There wasn't as much traffic as on the Indian highways. Nepal is smaller, less populated and less modernized than India.   However, it makes up for its less congested roads with narrow dirt roads and sheer cliff drop-offs, where you can see the remains of less fortunate vehicles far below.

We were shaken down by Maoist guerrillas on the way.   They stopped our car at gunpoint (machine guns, what else?) and demanded we pay a 'tax' of about $10.   We gladly handed over the cash.   Then, incredibly, the Maoists gave us a receipt for the extorted funds which we could show to other guerrillas to avoid double-paying if we were stopped again.   *How sporting of them!*

I was relieved when we arrived in Hetauda at last.   My foot was bruised from slamming down all day on phantom brakes.   My nerves were jagged from listening to the sound of our car scrambling for purchase on the sharp turns.   I felt like I'd been teetering on the edge of a cliff all day.

We were visiting a new partner agency, GWP, which runs programs to combat HIV/AIDS and human trafficking.   I knew GWP was helping survivors by offering them sustainable income making handmade paper. What I didn't know was that they also support sixty-one women's micro-finance groups in remote villages all over the region.   Every time we bought products from GWP, some of the funds went to help a rural women's group buy seeds, tools, or chickens.

Helping people in remote regions is challenging.   Many of the women GWP serves live an eight-hour walk away from their headquarters. We walked just a few hours to visit some of the closer villages.   It was hot and tempers became frayed.   Alicia became alarmingly red in the face (from heat exhaustion, not from anger), so we dropped her and Smarita back at the hostel to rest. Becky and I continued on with a representative from GWP.

As always, I loved spending time with the women. In one day, we were able to visit four different women's self-help groups. Each group had a different flavor, but they all had some things in common. Each group had fifteen to twenty members, aged twelve to twenty-five. They had all created small enterprises with micro-loans. The younger girls also attended school.

These were some of the most empowered women I have ever met. It was a privilege to sit with them, to hear about their small businesses, their hopes and dreams, and their challenges.

One fifteen-year-old girl, Fulmaya, had been rescued from an Indian circus after being enslaved for much of her childhood. After rescue, she had taken a small loan and started chicken farming to help her family. Fulmaya was in high school and interested in science. Her parents helped till her fields while she was at class. Because of Fulmaya's efforts, her family's financial situation had improved, ensuring that her younger sisters will not be trafficked. Together with her little sister, Fulmaya posed proudly for a photo in front of her chicken coop. That freedom-preserving chicken coop was the most beautiful agricultural enclosure I have ever seen!

Another group called 'Himchuli', which means mountain peak, used their loan to buy goats. These girls live in a stone quarry village, whose environment has been devastated by the quarry. Adults in the community can barely get by on their scant income from crushing rocks all day in the quarry. Thus, many had been forced or tricked into selling daughters into circus slavery or brothels.

When we visited, the girls, their parents, and it seemed the entire village gathered around to witness our meeting and to show their support. The girls had bought a computer and paid for a satellite link to create a community computer center. They plan to use the profits from their next project to build a new road and temple for the village. I was inspired by how empowered and proud they were.

By the time Becky and I got to the fourth village on our itinerary, it was dusk and we were worn out from hours of walking and three long, emotionally intense meetings. I felt the least I could offer these amazing women was my full attention and concentration. We didn't speak the same language, so we spoke through a translator, and communicated as best we could through earnest eye contact and nodding.

The women proudly walked us through the village, showing off their micro-enterprises - a small store and a large boar. At each of the previous villages, I had delivered a rousing speech congratulating the women on their entrepreneurial spirit and promising to help any way we could. By the time we got to village #4, I had lost my mojo entirely.

"Uh... you guys are great!" I lamely offered. "Really, great project...so impressed, so inspired...um..." Becky too was at a loss for words. Thankfully our translator and guide was able to recall and reconstruct some of the high points from my talks earlier in the day. He delivered a long and inspiring monologue on my behalf. The women in village #4 (which we later renamed Store and Boar village) must think English is an incredibly efficient language.

The trip ended as ridiculously as it began. Alicia and I flew home via Delhi, where the international and domestic terminals were five miles apart. There was supposedly a shuttle bus between the two, but I for one have never been able to find it, lo these many years.

Instead, we hailed a cab to get from the domestic to the international terminal. Being in a mad rush, we failed to notice that the cab was being driven by a boy of no more than fourteen, accompanied by his equally young friend, both high as kites. To add to the adventure, there was a huge diesel tank in the trunk. The diesel tank was so large, in fact, that the trunk would not close and our suitcases were at risk for spilling out onto the road.

Our young driver sped away from the curb and accelerated to sixty miles an hour, weaving dangerously through the traffic. "Please slow down!" I begged, then admonished, then shouted in fear. *Well, this is it,* I thought. *This is really the end of my life. We are driving with a crazed, drug-impaired teenager through busy residential streets (not a highway, mind you) at sixty miles an hour, with a huge diesel tank in the trunk. We are going to crash, the tank is going to explode and we are all going to die in a giant ball of flame.* I held Alicia's hand. We both thought sadly of our soon-to-be-motherless children.

To my surprise and relief, we made it to the international terminal alive and unharmed. I flung some rupees at the driver, appalled at his unsafe driving, before racing into the terminal to catch our flight.

We missed boarding the flight by two minutes. The next flight was leaving the next morning, eight hours later. Since we weren't allowed to check our bags or go to the gate until three hours before our flight, we spent a long, dark night of the soul huddled on the floor next to the ticket counters with all our suitcases.

That was not my finest hour. I found myself unable to rise above the situation. Sleeping was not recommended, what with the hard, bare floor and the need to watch over our luggage. Everything suddenly felt impossible. There were just too many obstacles. I became exceedingly cranky.

"Stupid taxi! Stupid airport! I hate this country," I grumbled. The many sad and difficult things we had seen on the trip were starting to catch up with me, and I was too weary to fend off the despair. This sometimes happens at the end of my trips.

Alicia eventually cajoled me out of my bad mood, and we spent the night laughing and talking. Again I was reminded how lucky I was to have such great friends willing to join me in this craziness. This is not the kind of work you could ever do alone.

24 FORGIVENESS

My work is built on close bonds, a foundation of love and fierce commitment. As closely as our team worked together, and as intense as the work could be, there were bound to be conflicts – conflicts aplenty. Like many women, I'm an accomplished conflict-avoider, so this has been one of the biggest challenges for me.

That spring, the new employment center in Calcutta was a primary focus of everyone's energy. The survivors had to learn how to run their lives independently for the first time - shopping, cooking, and budgeting their money. Becky, Smarita and Chan, who were co-managing the project, had to learn how to communicate across cultural barriers which were invisible, but strong as steel.

The center was first housed in an apartment we rented in the ground floor of Chan's house. We paid the rent and furnished the apartment, while Chan and his wife Debjani provided support to the young women after hours. Becky went to the center each day to supervise production and counsel the survivors.

The girls were giddy with their newfound freedom in a way that those of us have always been free cannot fully comprehend. They bought sewing machines, pots and pans, rugs and décor with the money we provided. They used their own earnings to buy groceries, and divided up the chores of cooking and cleaning. For the first time in their lives, the girls had control of their own money.

"No one tells me what to do now," said Mithu. "For the first time, I get to decide when to work, when to do housework or when to go to a film. When I get my paycheck, *I* get to choose whether to buy vegetables or a new sari".

For us, such simple choices seem trivial. *Buying vegetables, Woo hoo!* We have always had choices, so we take them for granted. The survivors, on the other hand, had grown up in poor village families. Continuous and tedious domestic labor was necessary for survival. It was demanded of all girls as soon as they could walk. Then they were trafficked into brothels where they were treated as less than human. In the brothels, no one cared what the girls wanted, how they felt, or even if they were in terrible pain. "In the brothel, you could scream as much as you wanted. Still no one would come," one of our girls once told me.

After rescue, the girls lived in a shelter, where they had to follow many rules and make many compromises to ensure the safety and comfort of a hundred other girls. There was a time for eating, a time for chores, a time for lights out. The shelter was surrounded by fences and high walls to keep out traffickers and to keep recently rescued girls from running away in the panic and confusion.

The new center was a transitional step between shelter dependence and independent living. It was also 'Real Life: Calcutta', fraught with adolescent drama. Although the girls were mostly in their early twenties, they had been robbed of their childhoods. Survivors are often emotionally delayed in the years following rescue. They have to make up the time they lost and to behave like teenagers before they can become adults, even if they are already past their teens in actual years.

The girls came into conflict with Chan and his wife, because they resented what they felt was interference. Chan and Debjani believed the girls still needed guidance and supervision. Becky got caught in the middle, since at age twenty-four, she was sometimes perceived by the girls as more of a peer than a boss.

One particularly tense week in March, the situation reached a boiling point, and Becky and Chan had a huge argument. It was so upsetting that Becky went home in tears. In their respective beds, both Becky and Chan tossed and turned all night in resentment and self-doubt.

Becky came to work exhausted the next morning. Debjani came straight down to greet her, and summoned her upstairs. Debjani had watched Chan tossing and turning all night, and she knew how important Chan and Becky's friendship was to both of them. Enough was enough, she decided.

Debjani's approach was a little unconventional, by Western or Indian standards. She called Becky and Chan over to her bed, and bade them sit on either side of her. Then she clutched each of their heads to her substantial bosom, where she held them tight, rocking slightly. At first it was sweet and affectionate, but after a few moments, when Becky tried to sit back up. Debjani held her fast.

"No, you guys are going to stay here until you work this out and forgive each other," she insisted. "You care about each other, and you are going to have to work this out".

As I said, Becky and Chan are stubborn, so it took eleven or twelve minutes for them to give in. Hats off to them! I would have caved a lot sooner. After two minutes I would be willing to say anything to get out of that awkward embrace. Long minutes passed, as the embrace went from sweet to awkward to downright absurd.

Becky suppressed a giggle. Then she began shaking with silent laughter. She and Chan talked through their differences, finding a resolution.

However, a few months later, it became clear that Chan's house was not the right place for the center. We decided to rent larger premises for it. Smarita and Becky took over the management of the project, and recruited ten more survivors from other shelter homes. They helped the young women to find and rent their own living quarters rather than living and working in the same place.

Some things were easier in the new location, but I was still surprised by how difficult and chaotic it was to set up a business for traumatized women in Calcutta. Something was always going haywire. At times it felt like all we did was put out fires (not literally).

Getting raw materials was a challenge. Dealing with the girls' trauma was a challenge. Raising money to pay the rent and the survivors' salaries was a challenge. I still wasn't great at fundraising, and a few times John and I had to tap into our own bank account to cover the costs.

We suddenly had a lot more products that we had to find a way to sell, and that was a continuing challenge for us in America. Working with partner shelters required a lot of finesse because they sometimes had different priorities and complicated chains of command. It was easy to get it wrong and offend someone by mistake.

However, the challenges we faced in those early days were nothing compared to the more serious conflicts to come, both in Asia and in the U.S. I was going to have to learn better ways of dealing with conflict or risk losing everything we had all worked so hard to create.

25 SHAKE YOUR BOOTY IN THE NAME OF JESUS

John and I danced around the living room, whooping loudly while the Reggae classic *'Shake your Booty in the Name of Jesus'* blasted on the stereo. After years of mounting financial stress, we finally had a breakthrough, and to that I just had to shake my booty in the name of the Lord. We had just received our first grant, enough to expand our programs, and to give me a salary after three years as a full-time volunteer.

I will always be thankful to that foundation - Humanity United - for believing in us, and giving us the practical help we needed to take our project to the next level. It had taken three years for us to get this first grant, but it was well worth it, which is why we were shaking our bootys (booties?) in the name of the Lord and howling with glee.

For exactly seven days, I walked around in a state of euphoria, a goofy smile plastered all over my face. I could barely contain myself. I stood up in church and announced the good news. It seemed like the whole town of Sandwich, Massachusetts rejoiced with me. But then...

26 A BAD BREAKUP

Having only days before been as happy as I had been in years, I was now as sad and discouraged as I had been in years. I had just lost one of my best friends. The break-up was with my dear friend Alicia and it seemed to come out of nowhere, knocking me flat.

In the past, whenever I had broken up with a guy, I saw it coming well before it happened. There is always a good possibility when you are dating that the relationship won't be life-long. Women's friendships, on the other hand, are supposed to last forever. Losing such a close friend felt like losing a piece of myself. I had never considered the possibility that Alicia and I would not be going through life together.

Alicia had joined me on my very first trip to India and on a subsequent trip to Nepal. She had hosted scores of home parties, and recruited others to do so. We had been extorted by Maoists together, for Pete's sake! For the past ten months, Alicia had been working at the charity in a managerial role. She was integrally involved in every aspect of the organization, and had played a major role in getting it off the ground.

Besides working together, we enjoyed a night out together with a group of other friends at least once a week. We hung out together with our kids, without kids, at the beach, or at her family's historic inn. I simply could not imagine this journey without Alicia. Now it seemed I was going to have to, because she was no longer speaking to me.

On the surface, the problem came down to money, but really it was about poor communication (mostly mine) and incompatible personalities (Alicia's and John's), and perhaps the fact that everyone had been doing too much for too long with too little. Resources were scarce and everyone was stretched thin.

Alicia was paid a small salary for her job at the charity. I did not realize that she was hoping for a full-time position and a more competitive salary once we got our first grant. This was not very clever of me. Since this first grant wasn't large enough to add or increase salaries for everyone, I thought the best approach was to add John and myself to the payroll as full-time employees, and keep Alicia on part-time. John and had used our savings to launch the charity, and were at the point where we needed to start earning in order to sustain our family.

Still, I should have known better than to assume it would be okay to make a major financial decision without talking openly to all concerned, well in advance of receiving the grant. Since my luck in obtaining any grants thus far had been poor, I wasn't confident we'd be receiving this one until just before the check arrived. I had made a rough budget, but had not figured out all the details, nor discussed the plan sufficiently with the team. By trying to avoid conflict, I mishandled the situation.

And while I'm speaking uncomfortable truths, here's another one: For many months, there had been a boiling cauldron of tension between John and Alicia which I had spent tremendous energy trying to mediate, gloss over, or ignore. It was inevitable that things would eventually bubble over, and when they did, they did so with a vengeance.

Alicia dropped by the house one Saturday, a few days after receiving news of the grant. I told her the happy news that I would be finally able to put myself on salary. She was stunned that I hadn't discussed this with her before. She was deeply hurt, and proceeded to quit and to storm out of the house. She slammed the door behind her, but not before saying some things that stung deeply. John actually had tears in his eyes by the end.

Maya and Luke crept in after Alicia left. "What was *that* about?!" they asked, surprised at all the shouting and door-slamming. I hardly knew what to say.

Several weeks and many emotionally loaded emails later, I was forced to conclude that this rift could not be repaired. I accepted my role in it, apologized, and with great sadness, accepted that the friendship was over.

Our close friends were in the awkward position of either choosing sides, or remaining friends with both of us and dividing their social lives accordingly. It was important to me that everyone understand my side of the story, and I talked everyone's ear off about it, until another friend counseled me that I had no control over what people thought. I needed to find my own truth and let go of the rest.

I tried to take this excellent advice, but for the next few months, I still awoke often in the night, fuming, guilty or hurt, or just wishing that things could go back to the way they were. Too many harsh words had been said, and too many open and honest words had *not* been said in advance of the incident.

I felt Alicia's absence not only in my personal life, but also at work. There was a gaping hole where her breezy confidence and wry sense of humor used to be. Also, she had been doing a lot of work, which I now had to take over. Things felt chaotic and overwhelming for a while. During that long time, my righteous indignation gradually dimmed, leaving a complicated combo platter of gratitude and remorse.

To start any ambitious project, you need the support and help of your friends and family, especially in the beginning. My dream would never have been realized without my friends and husband who threw themselves into the work alongside me. However, the people with you at the beginning are not always the people with you later on. There may come a time when friends become less available to help. They have to get on with other parts of their lives. And, as a project matures, you start to need more specialized, professional help that your friends might not be able to provide. This transition can be painful. It certainly was for me.

With my community of support fractured, Cape Cod no longer felt quite so wonderful. Meanwhile, John was increasingly suffering from seasonal affective disorder. He experienced a low-grade depression throughout the long gray winters, which seemed to be getting worse every year. Our cost of living was high. As the time when we had to move out of our house drew nearer, I began considering a more radical change of scenery.

27   TAZ'S TEN DOLLARS

Three months later, I was back in India. Taz, one of the survivors at our employment center, had been suffering for a year from a painful ovarian cyst which required surgery. Thanks to a good year of sales and the grant, we had the money to pay for it.

Taz was nineteen years old. She lived in a slum community with her brother and sister-in-law who were physically and verbally abusive. Because she had been trafficked, her position in the family was precarious. She was quiet and terribly fearful when she first came to us, but had matured into one of our most skillful artisans.

Through the previous months, Taz had been in pain. She came to work but was in too much pain to do much of anything. Becky and Smarita gave her a holiday bonus of 500 rupees ($10) because she wasn't able to earn a production bonus like the other women.

When I arrived in India, Becky told me about Taz's situation. We agreed to schedule her surgery immediately. On the morning of the operation, Becky and Smarita arrived early at the slum where Taz lived, near the railroad tracks.

Many girls disappear down those tracks from this desperately poor Muslim district. Girls have no voice, and little value apart from their relentless menial labor. In the worst cases, girls provide a source of income to the family through trafficking.

Taz was already waiting, out in the street, stooped from pain and clutching her stomach. In her hands she clutched the 500 rupees she had received as a holiday bonus. She insisted Becky take it as a contribution to her health care.

Becky tried to refuse. The gesture was thoughtful, but really wasn't necessary. Taz wouldn't take no for an answer. "You guys are paying for my operation," she insisted, "the least I can do is to contribute what I have to contribute!" You can be sure that those ten dollars were all the money Taz had in this world. All of her wages went to her living expenses and to help her family.

Ten dollars in the U.S. isn't terribly significant. It's two cups of premium coffee or half a paperback book, but for Taz, ten dollars was a small treasure because it gave her the opportunity to prove that she was not a victim. She was determined to contribute to the improvement of her own life and health, and not to be a charity case.

People are using many different approaches to deal with poverty, with slavery, and with human rights abuses all over the world, and I'm so glad of that. We need all hands on deck and many different ideas to solve the major problems in this world.

For my part, I'm glad to be taking the approach of rebuilding lives, of empowering women like Taz, through employment and education, to solve their own problems and build their own bright futures. Taz's empowering choice filled me with hope that this approach was working.

28 PAPER BAG PUPPETS AND BANANA LEAF PLATES

Sanlaap shelter: Twelve girls sat with us in a circle, afraid to move or speak. Two energetic volunteers, Paul and Susan, had just demonstrated how to make puppets out of paper bags, yarn and construction paper. Then we invited the girls to make their own puppets.

I gestured to the art supplies in the middle of the circle, smiled encouragingly, pointing at the blank paper bags and the finished samples. "Aekhon... Tomra Pala," I said in my halting preschool Bengali. Now it's your turn.

Nobody spoke or moved. This was becoming uncomfortable. I wondered if paper bag puppet-making was just too juvenile a project for this group of recently rescued twelve to fifteen year-olds. They had already experienced so much adult suffering, forced to dress as adults, to be used for sex by adult men.

The real problem turned out to be much simpler. These girls, who had been trafficked from remote rural villages in Nepal, were not comfortable with glue or scissors. They never had the chance to use them before.

We had been invited to paint and furnish a preschool for the children of survivors at Sanlaap shelter. Traffickers use babies as a means to subjugate their mothers and keep them from running away. Because of this history, the mothers were hesitant to leave their babies in the care of others. This was a problem because survivors with children need to take advantage of the child care at the shelter in order to attend school or work.

Sanlaap's founder, the late Indrani Sinha, was always looking for new ways to help the girls in her care. It was her idea to create a space so beautiful and inviting, it would inspire the young mothers to leave their children there.

For our extreme shelter make-over, we enlisted the help of twenty-five survivors living at the shelter, including some young tribal Nepali girls, who had been rescued only a month before from a particularly distressing situation. These girls were still highly traumatized. They spoke Tamang - a tribal language– rather than Nepali. Nepal has 125 tribal languages. It is impossible for the shelter counselors to speak all of these languages, and nobody at Sanlaap at that time spoke Tamang.

Girls are trafficked from all over South Asia to the major cities in India. The fact that they can't understand the language when they first arrive at a brothel makes it easy for traffickers to control them and impossible for them to escape.

When this group of Tamang girls was rescued, they were terrified that they were going to be betrayed and trafficked again. A few days before we came to the shelter, the girls had been driven to a court date. On the way home, the driver stopped at a truck stop so they could have some tea and use the bathroom. The girls became terribly agitated and began sobbing. It turned out many of them had been exploited out of a truck stop brothel. They were convinced they were about to be sold again and left at the truck stop.

The lack of common language made everything harder and more complicated. The girls hadn't yet been able to receive counseling in their own language. They hung out in their small group of fellow Tamang girls, isolating themselves from the other survivors at the shelter.

Fortunately, for the two weeks I was there, we were able to bring a native Tamang speaker to translate. On our first day at Sanlaap, we went out into the courtyard with her to invite the Tamang girls to join us. We approached a group of ten girls, who were sitting, as was their custom, in a tight circle far from everyone else. They looked somber and painfully young. The youngest was eleven. The oldest was fifteen.

When our translator Rangita approached them, the girls recoiled ever so slightly, closing ranks, becoming visibly anxious, looking down or away. When she spoke to them in their own language, their faces broke into the most amazing smiles, a mixture of surprise, joy, and enormous relief. It was one of the most profound moments of human connection I have ever seen. It was the first time these girls had heard an adult speaking their language in years.

Rangita sat and talked with the girls for half an hour and then they began venturing, by twos and threes, up to our workspace. At first they were reserved, their faces blank and unreadable, but then a few girls picked up paintbrushes and set to work on the preschool renovation. The rest joined us in the awkward paper bag puppet circle. Thankfully, once we showed them how to use the glue and scissors, they threw themselves into the puppet-making with tremendous enthusiasm and creativity.

Over the next two weeks, I witnessed a gradual inner and outer transformation. The girls painted with ever-increasing speed and enthusiasm. They delved into our art projects, their creativity flourishing with ever more elaborate designs.

As the room was transformed from a dingy, cluttered storeroom into a lovely preschool, the girls were gradually changing as well. They were still deeply traumatized, but sometimes I saw them laughing. They were still wounded, but showing signs of healing, still afraid, but taking steps toward trusting. Anjali would slip her hand in mine while we painted, side by side. Saloni began taking charge of the supplies at the beginning and end of each day.

Of course the art projects and our loving support were not responsible for all of the girls' progress. Nonetheless, I felt blessed to play a small part in it, to be there at that precise moment in time to see a miracle unfolding.

On our last day, we inaugurated the beautiful new schoolroom with a ceremony and ice cream party. This being India, there was much pomp and circumstance, and many speeches. My voice was raw from exhaustion and too much talking. I looked a fright with my hair hanging in limp strands and huge dark circles under my eyes, but in all the pictures of me that day, I am glowing with joy.

As I cleaned up the room and prepared to leave on the final day, I found a small note tucked into a can of paintbrushes:

'Please take my love and don't forget me. I always remember you in my heart. I love you all so much. God bless you... With love, Anjali'.

As inspiring as it was to work with girls like Anjali and to see them beginning to heal, I also reached the limits of my own ability to cope on that trip. At one point, I actually fainted over a plate of eggs in a restaurant. I was exhausted and emotionally drained, but there was much to do. Several of our volunteers were ill and one ended up in the hospital. On the bright side, I found the perfect metaphor for the situation: wet banana leaf plates.

When we visit or work at shelter homes, we are always given lunch, which is so nice. The food at Sanlaap was simple - rice and lentils which we ate with our fingers (not as easy as it sounds - the lentils are liquidy), served on these environmentally awesome plates made out of dried banana leaves.

One day that week, the banana leaf plates had just been washed (in unfiltered water from the retaining pond) and were still beaded with water. Of course the water in India can wreak havoc on our foreign stomachs. So the look on our team members' faces as their food was spooned onto those wet plates was a priceless combination of disbelief, fear, and finally resignation. We were really hungry, appreciative of the effort, and too tired to explain, so we just went for it, despite our fears. And happily, that day, there were no negative repercussions.

29 BIHAR

Many times doing since I began this work, I've been in situations where I thought, just for a moment or two, that I was about to die, or that someone else on my team was at risk for his or her life. Most often, this was a highway driving situation. Now, for the first time, the risk was all too real.

After the first few trips, some volunteers regretted the fact that they didn't have time to see more positive and culturally rich aspects of India. This was a good point. There is so much more to India than poverty and oppression.

Varanasi, in Northern India, is an ancient city of temples on the Ganges River. It is a Hindu pilgrimage site and a once-in-a-lifetime tourism experience. We decided to take our volunteers up to Varanasi to give them a break from the relentless pace (and wet banana leaf plates) of the work in Calcutta. We were excited to share some of India's cultural richness, and to visit a new partner organization – MSEMVS - which helps entire communities get out of bonded labor slavery.

Bonded labor is a very common form of slavery in South Asia, affecting millions of people. In bonded labor slavery, individuals or entire families perform backbreaking work for no pay, to work off 'debts'. Often these are small debts of less than $100 which accumulate over time because the system is designed to keep people enslaved.

Generations of a family can become trapped in a cycle of slavery and steadily accruing debt. Threats of violence, or actual violence, serve to keep them enslaved, and many are not even aware that bonded labor is an illegal practice.

Sojourner Truth once said 'I freed a thousand slaves, and I could have freed a thousand more, if only they knew that they were slaves'. She could have been talking about people in bonded labor, because they do not consider themselves to be slaves. They have been told throughout their lives that it is their legal and moral obligation to pay off their debts in the only way they know how.

Children who grow up in bonded labor slavery do not get an education or learn basic life skills, so as adults they are vulnerable to every kind of exploitation. This is how the cycle of abuse continues from generation to generation.

As a parent, it was hard for me to imagine. What if every single day, instead of putting my kids on a school bus, I sent them off to crush rocks in the blistering sun?

MSEMVS has created a system that frees entire villages from bonded labor slavery. First, they set up a school and convince families to allow their children to attend the school for six hours a day rather than working. They use the school as a headquarters from which to educate the adults in the community about their rights. They teach people that bonded labor is a form of slavery, that it is illegal, and that no one is obliged to work as a slave to pay off debts.

After months of advocacy, when enough community members are ready, the entire village leaves slavery as a group. This way, no single family can be targeted for reprisals. With ongoing support from MSEMVS, the freed villagers organize and begin advocating for their own rights at the district and state level.

I was intrigued by this innovative approach, and looked forward to going to Varanasi with the team, but when the time came, it just wasn't possible for me to leave Calcutta. There was still a lot to be done to finish remodeling the pre-school, and I was working with the team on a large order at the employment center. I was also setting up a school sponsorship program for the children in the Kidderpore red light area.

To be completely honest, I was also exhausted and irritable. The volunteers weren't particularly needy or demanding, but get any group of twelve people together and make them work ten hours a day in Calcutta, you're going to have to field a lot of questions and deal with many small crises. Mothering both the survivors and the volunteers under such stressful circumstances was taxing, and people were starting to get on my nerves, a sure sign I was overdoing the togetherness.

I asked Dan, a veteran volunteer on his second trip, and Sudebi, one of our Indian staff members, to lead the volunteers on the trip to Varanasi. We arranged overnight train travel for the group in sleeper cars. They were to arrive in Varanasi in the morning and stay at a pleasant hotel, from which they could enjoy some tourism. On the second day, they would meet with MSEMVS, travel out to one of the freed villages, and then take the train back to Calcutta in the evening. It was a good plan, I thought, short and sweet.

Unfortunately, it turned out to be neither.

I had drilled the volunteers on public health guidelines for the excursion. "Don't drink anything which might contain water! Don't eat anything that could have been washed in water! Stay away from dairy products! Don't eat street food! Eat pre-packaged foods such as nuts or chips. And for God's sake, whatever you do, don't eat the food they sell on the train!"

I must have been using my mom voice when I said this, because the response of some of the volunteers was exactly what I would expect from my kids: they assumed my warnings were an overprotective rant and were determined to find out for themselves, the hard way.

At the train station, one volunteer bought a fruit smoothie and shared it with several others. Another bought and consumed a sandwich. These two hadn't been sick yet, after a week in Calcutta, so perhaps they were feeling extra-hearty. Or maybe they were feeling as irritable as I was, and ordered the smoothies and sandwich to prove Mom wrong. Nasty bacteria rowed merrily, merrily, merrily, merrily into their digestive tracts despite whatever they were thinking.

It was a long, dark night of the soul for the Varanasi contingent. The train, which was supposed to take twelve hours, chug-chugged along for eighteen. Four volunteers were violently ill, forced to brave the truly appalling conditions of the train bathrooms. Those who were not ill tried to help the sick ones. By the time they arrived in Varanasi, three volunteers were dangerously dehydrated, so Dan called for a doctor to meet them at the hotel.

It was fair to assume that an Indian doctor would be familiar with food-borne bacterial diseases. To the doctor's credit, he did give the sickies a shot which stopped their vomiting. Then, inexplicably, he told them that they had contracted 'cold sickness', which he claimed, is a common illness caused by drafts from the open train windows (?)

After the treatments, and some rest, everyone began to feel better, and the group was able to enjoy a day of tourism. They visited the magnificent temples, practiced yoga on the hotel roof deck, and recovered from the indignities of the train ride.

The next day they were supposed to meet MSEMVS early in the morning, so that they would have time to drive out to the formerly enslaved villages and meet survivors. I was very surprised to receive a call from Sudebi at 10:00, informing me that the volunteers had decided *not* to visit MSEMVS. Instead they had all gone out shopping. This was very surprising, and embarrassing, since the MSEMVS staff and villagers had been eagerly awaiting our visit for weeks. This choice seemed out of character for the volunteers, who had wanted to spend every free minute at the shelters in Calcutta, barely stopping to rest or eat. It just didn't make sense.

My confusion only increased as the day wore on. The decisions of the volunteers in Varanasi became more and more erratic, leading those of us in Calcutta to wonder if they had been smoking ceremonial hookahs, or if the food poisoning had caused a mass hysteria.

The train back to Calcutta was due to leave at 6:00 pm and I couldn't wait to hear that my friends were safely aboard it. Alas, at 5:30, Dan called to report that the volunteers had been so traumatized by their train journey, they had decided to rent two SUVs and drive back to Calcutta rather than enduring another train voyage. Driving from Varanasi to Calcutta takes at least twenty-four hours, much of it over derelict roads. Worse yet, the route from Varanasi leads through the most dangerous parts of Bihar.

The state of Bihar is a state in crisis. It is underdeveloped and often lawless, with an appallingly high incidence of trafficking, ritual murder, child marriage, intergenerational slavery, violence against women, violence against everyone, banditry, and exploitation of low caste and tribal people. Seriously, it's a rough place.

The volunteers' route was to take them through Bihar's 'Forest of Grimaldi' in the middle of the night. Even the name sounds ominous. Bandits lay out nails to cause flat tires or car crashes. Once you stop, the bandits come out of their hiding places in the woods to rob you, or worse.

Back in Calcutta, I was holding a vigil with Becky and Smarita at Becky's apartment. We called Dan and Sudebi and tried to convince them to abort their plan to drive through Bihar. Unfortunately, they were already en route and stubbornly convinced that their plan was a good one.

Here's a better plan: get on the train and heed the warnings about food consumption - prepackaged only!

Smarita urged me to ask the volunteers to stop driving until morning. Apart from anything else, their drivers had already been up and working for fifteen hours. It didn't seem safe for these men to drive another twenty hours with no sleep. And then there was the whole Forest of Grimaldi issue. We feared for the volunteers' lives and safety.

The party consisted of two men, four gorgeous young women, two middle-aged women, and one person whose gender identity was unconventional enough to create a particular target in Bihar, a very traditional society. I did not think much of the group's chances in any kind of attack.

The team was hell-bent on driving on, despite my protests. A major argument ensued, conducted over several hours in hurried cellphone installments from various truck stops across Uttar Pradesh and Bihar. Meanwhile, night fell.

"Let me talk to Dan", I said. "Dan, you guys have to stop," I implored him. "YOU ARE GOING TO DIE!" I admit, this was a bit dramatic, but Smarita was standing in front of me insisting that the volunteers might very well die if they continued this ill-considered plan.

For some reason, the exhausted group had become so desperate to return to Calcutta, and so averse to another night on the train, they simply would not be deterred.

Dan tried to convince the group to stop for the night, but hotter heads prevailed. "Let me talk to Linda", I tried next. Linda was a serene and level-headed grandmother who had been working for us in India for three months already. Surely *she* would listen to reason. Linda responded calmly but could not convince the others to stop. They were convinced that we were just being melodramatic and were mistaken about the danger.

Meanwhile, their drivers were telling them it was perfectly safe. Of course the drivers had their own reasons for wanting to continue. They had negotiated a set rate for the fifty-hour round trip, and had nothing to gain from delays.

Waiting between calls, Becky and I relieved our stress by choreographing a dance number about the situation. I know it sounds inappropriate, but it did relieve the stress. Earlier that day, we had bought two enormous rolls of foam for padding handbags. We hid behind the rolls of foam to play the role of the Grimaldi Forest bandits.

We were veering wildly between distress and hysterical laughter when the team called again, this time to propose a compromise. They had stopped at a gas station, and the owner had suggested that they could sleep outside in the courtyard (!) Nightmare visions of the team's demise flashed before me.

"Are you guys insane?!" I demanded. "Do you seriously think it's safe to sleep outside at a gas station in Bihar?!!"

"But they have cots for us," the volunteers calmly explained. Visions of the naïve volunteers, sleeping peacefully in their cots while bandits silently surrounded them, flashed before me. I pulled out all the stops.

"Guys, I may be wrong. I may be crazy, but I need you to do this for me. People offering to let you sleep outside their gas station cannot be trusted! This smells like a trap. Gather your belongings and leave now. Drive at least an hour, then find a hotel. Call the police and tell them where you are and where you are headed. Gather together in one hotel room and lock the door. Wait until morning before you begin driving again".

Some of the volunteers were furious. They did not agree that they were in any danger. They were exhausted and intensely frustrated at having to waste six hours waiting around a hotel room.

In the end, they grudgingly agreed to get a hotel room, and left at around 4:00 in the morning. They arrived safely in Calcutta late that day. I can't convey how happy I was to lay eyes on those cranky, disheveled men and women. After a shower and a few beers, they mostly got over their irritation. That night, as we sat in a circle sharing our joys and challenges from our two weeks in Calcutta, I couldn't stop counting heads.

Twelve. Dodged a bullet on that one.

30 RICH SANDY THOMPSON

When I was growing up in suburban Detroit, there was a girl at my church named Sandy Thompson. Sandy was twenty years old when I was fifteen but we were both in tenth grade because Sandy had been the victim of ritual abuse and severe neglect for most of her childhood. Until the age of twelve, Sandy was raised in a remote cabin with her nine brothers and sisters. None of them attended a single day of school, and all were abused, as Sandy described it, 'in every way'.

Sandy and her adoptive parents were very open and matter-of-fact about her history. They were determined not to let it become a dark secret for people to gossip about. They demystified the abuse, and put the shame where it belonged, not on Sandy but on those who had hurt her, and those who had known the family but had not bothered to look beneath the surface.

When Sandy was twelve, she and her brothers and sisters were rescued and adopted. Sandy had to start kindergarten as a twelve-year-old, just like many of the survivors in our program. She worked hard and made steady progress, eventually graduating high school and even going to college, despite some learning issues resulting from her late start and trauma.

Sandy had an odd manner, as you might expect, but I fiercely admired her. She had suffered a horrific childhood, full of pain and fear. Her adoptive parents were sweet, simple, and devout, but they had fifty kinds of nothing. They lived in a trailer home with Sandy and their two biological children.

Sandy was not even five feet tall. Years of malnutrition had stunted her growth. Life was likely to hold many challenges for our Sandy, but she refused to be pitied.

If you ever sympathetically said, *'poor Sandy'*, even if you meant nothing by it, like if Sandy had a big exam the next day, or had a bad cold, she would practically shout the retort "I'm NOT poor, I'm rich in the Lord!". It became a catch phrase for the rest of us. We loved it, and we loved our feisty, Lilliputian Sandy for her absolute refusal to become an object of pity.

I've told my Sandy story a hundred times. I still like to channel her, in my own darker moments.

I'm NOT poor. I'm rich in the Lord!

35   RICH IN THE LORD?

Diary Entry, Palm City, Florida: *'Where the heck is Palm City, Florida and why, oh why am I living here? We are renting a small (beige) house identical to the scores of others in a gated neighborhood. Outside, everything is beige. I hate that porridgey non-color more than ever! Inside, our house looks like a cheap motel decorated in the eighties. Remember teal and fuchsia? I am oppressed by those colors in every direction. Teal carpets, teal and fushsia striped wallpaper. Floor to ceiling mirrors in the master bathroom. Monstrous!*

The neighbors around us in every direction are u elderly people, not the nice kind who bring cookies. I have not met a single potential friend in the five months we have lived here. Are you there, God? It's me, Sarah. Please get me out of here!'

Somehow the previous winter, I had gotten the idea that it would be fun, rejuvenating, and in every way good for our family and organization to move to Florida. Some months earlier, while attending a conference in Fort Lauderdale, I had felt compelled to skip out of the workshop and take a walk on the beach. It was 84 degrees and brilliant sunshine, with a lovely sea breeze blowing. I reveled in every sun-kissed moment. When I got home, I mentioned casually to John, "Imagine if we lived in Florida…"

John had longed to move to Florida for years, enticed by the climate, the relaxed lifestyle, the fishing, and the low cost of living. Running a nonprofit in Massachusetts was expensive, with its higher taxes, higher salaries, and higher cost of living, and we no longer had a nest egg that we could tap whenever the charity ran short.

Perhaps the most compelling reason for a move was that John had come to dread the long gray winters of New England. He felt the climate steadily chipping away at his health and joie de vivre. He had been nudging me for years to consider moving somewhere sunnier. Once that cat was out of the bag, there was no stuffing it back in.

That very night, we were looking at Florida towns online, comparing schools and available rental homes. Perhaps the decision was just a little rash, but I've always loved an adventure. I was sure it would work out wonderfully.

Six months later, we loaded up our cars and left the Cape, after twelve years of building a life there. This was the place where we started our family and bought our first house. This was where we launched our charity, and where I grieved the loss of my parents. I had found a community of friends and supporters on the Cape who pulled me through rough times and joined in the celebration of every success. It was an awful lot to leave behind, but John's needs were just as important.

For several months that spring, I packed and organized our home and office, lightening our load by half. I was forced to go through all the boxes of my parent's belongings, a lifetime of letters and photos, diplomas, and souvenirs. I had been putting this off for years, and with good reason. It made me inexpressibly sad. I was in no mood to confront my lingering grief while also preparing a cross-country move, but it had to be done. We were moving from an enormous six-bedroom house with attic, to a three-bedroom rental with barely any storage space.

As money was tight, we opted to rent a large truck and pack it ourselves, with the help of some friends. *Note to everyone over the age of 25: Don't do this!* I'm surprised I still have those friends. When the morning of the move came, we had not dealt with the eight thousand final details of move-out, so we were faced with an enormous amount of work yet to do. The new homeowners were arriving that afternoon. Under extreme stress, we packed up our last remaining belongings, cleaned the house, and took truckloads of garbage to the town dump.

Luke, who was then eight and had a disposition of sunshine and silliness, got really upset and started crying and actually hitting his head against the wall in frustration. I dropped the kids at a friend's house, dripping with guilt about the stress that my impulsive comment, "*What if we moved to Florida?*" had created. Finally, at 1:00 pm, we pulled out. By this point, even our dog was a panting, nervous wreck. I felt more than a little sorry for myself too.

When we finally arrived in Florida two days later, I put the stress of the move behind me, and set about building my beautiful new life.

Into every life a little rain must fall. I know it. I believe it. Nonetheless, I was shocked at how unhappy I felt those first few months in Florida. It didn't take long for me to realize that we had chosen the absolute wrong place for me. I was physically present in Palm City, but I didn't, nor would I ever belong there, and neither would my children.

Perhaps if a person lived in Palm City long enough, she could find nice friends and build a community, but there were no obvious places to start. There were no coffee shops, music venues, or local artisan galleries. I could find no hiking clubs, or friendly mom's groups. I couldn't find a church that met my needs spiritually or socially. I joined a women's club and found it prissy.

Dropping the kids off at school one morning, I was dumbstruck by how blonde everyone was. I thought Florida was going to be more diverse than the Cape, but apparently not Palm City. Even though my own kids happened to be blonde, it still annoyed me. The more time passed, the stronger became my intense, visceral dislike of the town.

Without the support and distraction of my community on Cape Cod, my work began to feel overwhelming too. In Sandwich I was practically famous. Many people knew me and knew about our work, which made it easy to get volunteers when we needed help. In Palm City, I was not only lonely, I was completely anonymous. I began to worry that I had destroyed my beautiful life.

The children were equally unhappy. Luke was having a hard time at his new school and had no friends. He said the boys only judged you on how far you could throw a baseball, and he apparently couldn't throw it far enough. He played alone at recess every day, pretending not to mind. His sunny demeanor became more clouded, more reserved, which greatly troubled me. Maya, now ten years old, was desperately homesick for the Cape, and at least once a week, she cried for an hour or two before bedtime, begging us to move back.

I would have loved to! Unfortunately, it wasn't that easy. John was blissfully happy for the first time in years. He couldn't imagine moving back to New England, where his seasonal affective disorder had made him so miserable.

One night in October, I invited John to join me on a walk around the block. I confessed how unhappy I was feeling. It did not go well. John was appalled. He felt I had not given our new hometown nearly enough time and was being grossly unfair. My intuition told me that no longer how long I stayed, I would never find a true home in Palm City. My once wonderful life had been in a tailspin ever since we got there.

My low spirits were aggravated by my awareness that I had brought these problems on myself. I berated myself for making the wrong decision, causing myself and my children to be so unhappy. Now we were stuck in Palm City, and there seemed to be no way to reverse the decision without causing John to suffer.

Feeling trapped, and having no idea how to fix the problem, I became increasingly depressed. Back in New England, I used to go out several nights a week, with friends, to choir or pottery class. Now I stayed home every night, working or numbing my mind with television.

Things were difficult for many reasons that year, not just because I was homesick and hated our new town. The economic downturn had begun to affect us. Sales and donations were down. We were between grants and found ourselves without enough money to sustain our growing programs.

I hadn't done nearly enough to raise funds over the previous three years, choosing instead to focus on building programs for the survivors. Now we had all these wonderful programs that cost money every month to operate, and not nearly enough funds to go around.

Any more mistakes I've made want to come kick me while I'm down?

I noticed that all our staff meetings now centered on the same depressing theme: "Have you looked at our numbers?" (John). Of course I hadn't. I wasn't naturally a numbers person and tended to blind optimism. "Sales are down, donations are down. At this rate, we'll be completely out of cash in two months. We simply do not have enough money for all these programs".

We had this discussion every other day for three or four months. Tempers became frayed. It drained the joy from my work. We decided to stop paying John altogether. Our family could squeak by on my salary, but the drop in income would make it that much harder to afford another move. We couldn't afford office space either, so we worked from our tiny house, which was another entirely dysfunctional situation. I was annoyed at John, yet I could never get more than five feet away from him. It was claustrophobic and distracting.

With each passing week, I felt more and more like a huge failure. I woke up almost every night in the wee hours to ruminate about my miserable living situation and our financial woes. Often I ended up sleeping on the couch so I could be alone with my angst, or to pray for deliverance. Sometimes I just felt so frustrated, I needed to sleep alone.

For the first time, I began to question whether I could continue running the charity. I fantasized about bundling the kids in the car and driving away, anywhere, with or without my husband. My relentless hope was wavering.

In December, we drove up to New England for Christmas. As soon as we arrived on the Cape, there was a big snowstorm, turning every quaint little street into a picture postcard. Standing in line at the convenience store in my old neighborhood, I felt a rush of calm and happiness for the first time in six months. *Home at last.*

Sadly, my euphoric mood did not last, because John fell immediately into a dreadful funk. The lack of light was intolerable to him, he claimed. I secretly doubted that seasonal affective disorder could be triggered that quickly, and suspected that he was just afraid I would want to move back to the Cape. Of course that is exactly what I wanted! For the first time in our twelve years of marriage, the two of us wanted entirely different things, things that were in fact mutually exclusive. For once in my life, I did not have a plan, and this made me profoundly uncomfortable.

John and I tried to muddle through our conflict and morose moods to create a happy holiday for the kids. Of course, pretending only made us feel worse. Maya spent a weekend with friends, but when we picked her up, she broke down in sobs and once again begged us to move back to the Cape. She expressed her misery as only a ten-year-old can, with absolute conviction and maximum drama. Luke sat mutely, refusing to state any opinion whatsoever.

My friends were sympathetic, but I could tell some of them felt that my problems were the inevitable result of my own unwise decisions and rash moves. "Couldn't John go back to working in finance?" a few friends cautiously suggested. "Then you guys would have the money to live wherever you want".

Of course, I had thought of that, but the charity was hard enough to run with both of us working full time. John's business and technical expertise were vital to the organization's survival. In any case, he had no interest in going back to a career finance. He had come to love our work with survivors as much as I did.

After five days of uneasy détente, we headed up to New Hampshire, to spend Christmas with close friends. Once we got to a place where we felt really comfortable, and didn't need to pretend things were okay, tensions gradually began to ease.

"Maybe we could go to grad school and teach at a college?" I suggested to John one night as we lay in bed. "Or we could find a sunny place to live in the mountains, like North Carolina or Colorado... Whatever we do, we have to get out of our black and white thinking, as if our only options are Florida or Cape Cod, running our nonprofit and being perpetually broke, or giving it up entirely and having you return to banking".

We stayed up late that night, considering a variety of crazy options, and gradually feeling more optimistic. We were thinking as partners again, rather than adversaries. By the end of the trip, we had agreed to leave Palm City when school let out in June, and in the meantime, to search for a new place to live where we could both be happy.

Armed once again with a game plan, the long drive home was less fraught. Now all we had to do was find a new hometown, get the charity on solid financial footing so John could go back on salary, come up with some cash for another move, and help the kids adjust to the idea of another new home and new school. Granted, it was still a bit daunting, but at least it was a plan.

36 AND NOW FOR SOMETHING COMPLETELY DIFFERENT

January, 2010: I stood in the dark shack, sweating in the 120 degree heat. The corrugated metal door and roof provided little in the way of protection from the elements, but on the bright side, there were some large holes in the brick walls which provided a sort of low-tech ventilation – along with a disheartening view of the red light area just outside… I squinted at Paul through the darkness, trying to gauge his reaction. Was this really going to be the location of our new workshop?

A trip to India in January was just the break I needed from my personal problems. Becky had just announced her intention to return to the U.S. for graduate school in the spring. Becky had been serving in Calcutta for two and a half years by then, and had developed deep relationships with our survivors and partners. She was fluent in Bangala. She dressed and ate like a native Calcuttan. She drank water right from the tap! (*note to everyone who is not Becky: Do not try this!*) She knew her way around every red light area and shelter home and wholesale market in the city.

Becky had played a pivotal role in launching our programs in India. We needed to find a replacement to oversee our programs there, but it was going to be tough to find someone as talented and as full of love as Becky.

We found the perfect candidate in Paul, one of our strongest trip volunteers (and a veteran of the ill-fated Bihar trip). Paul had dreamed of returning to India and working for Made By Survivors ever since his trip the year before. Right after he got home from that trip, Paul had been laid off from his job. It seemed like a disaster at the time, but it opened up a path in his life that he might not have discovered otherwise.

In January, 2010, we hired Paul as our Asia Program Director, and he moved to Calcutta to begin a whole new life. His presence there would ultimately create the opportunity for hundreds of survivors to also enjoy a beautiful new life.

As a former District Manager at The Body Shop, overseeing dozens of stores and hundreds of employees, Paul brought much-needed expertise in retail and human resources. He began building a super-efficient local team in Calcutta. First he hired Doel, a brilliant young Bengali woman who had just finished her master's degree in business administration. Then he added Soma, a woman from a poor village family who been denied opportunities and education in her childhood, and was passionate about making sure our girls had every possible opportunity in their lives. We originally hired Soma as a translator, but her exceptional talents and saintly nature soon became apparent, so Paul promoted her to Program Manager.

On my visit to India that January, I met my own mentor and role model, Aloka Mitra (uh-lō-kah mēe-tra). Aloka is the founder of Women's Interlink Foundation, a network of eighty programs – shelter homes for survivors, red light drop in centers, rural development programs, train platform schools, homes for destitute seniors, the disabled, and more. She conducts her own rescues through her relationships in the red light area. Mothers, aunts and neighbors alert Aloka when a young girl is about to be trafficked, or has recently been brought in to one of the brothels.

Aloka has been working in this field for over thirty years, and is now in her sixties. She still has more energy than anyone I have ever met. While Paul and I would be falling asleep on our feet after a twelve-hour day with Aloka, she would always have energy to burn. "Let's go out for dinner!" she would suggest gaily at 9:00 pm, and we'd end up merrymaking for another three or four hours.

Aloka routinely works these twelve hour days, charging around West Bengal overseeing her many projects. She still finds the time to sit and truly listen to each girl, to inquire about the small details of each child's life, her schooling, her dreams or her health. She brings incredible gentleness and humor to each interaction.

When Aloka directed her radiant personality towards me, it felt like being bathed in sunshine. In some ways, it felt like having a mother again, someone I could turn to for advice and guidance. With all the hundreds of survivors and other desperate cases in need of Aloka's attention and care, I felt almost guilty taking any for myself, but it felt so good to be nurtured by her loving energy.

As our partnership grew, Aloka welcomed us to bring volunteers and to run programs at her two Calcutta shelter homes. That January, we painted murals all over her Nijloy shelter, and launched a school sponsorship program for her girls there. I soon felt as if that shelter was my second home. I was so comfortable and happy there.

Not everything in India was flowing so smoothly, however. At the Destiny Center, we were facing some difficult decisions. John and I strongly believed that we should change the focus of the Destiny Center from sewing to silver jewelry. Jewelry was our most popular product type and we knew we could sell it more easily than bags or anything else.

Shifting to silver jewelry production would also allow us to pay a higher wage to survivors. We were confident it would be more profitable, and therefore more sustainable for our organization.

Smarita, who was managing the Destiny Center, disagreed. She still saw a lot of potential in a sewing-based center, and thought it would be a waste of time and resources to switch to jewelry after a year and a half training survivors in sewing. She and Becky had put a tremendous amount of time and energy into the Destiny Center and had strong opinions about what was best for it. We all did.

Becky, ever the diplomat, saw the merits of both sides, and just wanted everyone to be happy. She felt terribly torn and stressed by the whole uncomfortable business.

After months of heated discussions and soul-searching, we finally agreed that the best solution was for the Destiny Center to become independent of Made By Survivors, with Smarita as its sole director. We would launch a whole new center for jewelry.

On the bright side, this took the pressure off me for raising the several thousand dollars it cost every month to maintain the Destiny Center. However, I was sad that we couldn't all move forward together, and that I had to let go of a project to which I felt such a strong attachment. It had been a flagship project, our first independent program in Asia.

The Destiny Center went on to grow and thrive, and Smarita continues to do a wonderful job leading it, but at the time the situation was fraught with tension, and left me with a lingering sense of loss and frustration.

This was another time where I learned a crucial lesson through a painful experience. As with my blow-up with Alicia, I had once again failed to communicate succinctly at the beginning. I had known that tensions were mounting for some months. Something needed to be said, but by the time I finally got up the nerve to say it, I, and everyone else involved, was too angry and upset to have a rational discussion.

I finally got the message that winter that my own behaviour was contributing to painful situations in my work, and changed my conflict-avoiding ways once and for all. I'm happy to report that my working relationships have hugely improved as a result.

Painful as it was to let go of the Destiny Center after investing so much in it, we were able to help even more survivors by doing so. Smarita continued to employ survivors at Destiny, and added more women to her team over time. We started the jewelry program and empowered a whole new group of survivors that way.

Launching the new program to train survivors as metalsmiths proved to be our biggest challenge yet. Our vision was to offer high-skills training that would elevate the survivors' status in society. The training would lead to high-paying jobs that would pull them well out of poverty. This career path could earn survivors a middle class salary comparable to a teacher or civil servant.

We knew we could sell hand-made silver jewelry for a good price in America, enabling us to pay the survivors handsomely. In order to make high quality silver jewelry, the women would need several years of intensive training and practice. I knew that developing such expertise and having an outlet for their creativity would do wonders for their self-esteem.

At the beginning, neither I, nor anyone on the team had the slightest idea how to make silver jewelry, how to teach it, or what equipment we would need. We reached out to our online community, and found someone who could tell us.

Melissa Tyson is a successful art jeweler in North Carolina. She had invited me and Paul to her house for a crash course in silver jewelry fabrication in the fall of 2009. Then she designed some fairly simple pieces that the survivors could learn to make with six months of training.

Melissa was expecting a baby, so she couldn't travel to India to conduct the training herself. We tried and failed to find a female trainer in India. Metalsmithing in India has historically been done only by men.

We were greatly blessed to find Dianna Badalament, a jeweler from the Bay Area who was available to travel and train overseas. Thankfully, Dianna turned out to be not just a great jeweler and designer, but also a natural counselor and problem-solver. She became the heart and soul of our India Jewelry Program.

Before we could send Dianna to Calcutta to begin the training, we needed a workspace. Becky had scouted and put down a deposit on a location for us in the Kidderpore red light area. During my trip in January, Paul and I made the trip to Kidderpore to see the new workshop. We were taken aback by the condition of the building. I thought it looked like a hovel from the sixteenth century, a place where a poor beggar might go to drink himself to death. Rental properties in the red light area are expensive and hard to come by, but still...

Neither of us could imagine running a program in this run-down shack. The heat alone would be unbearable. The location, right smack in the middle of 'the lanes', would be convenient for the women living in that community, but depressing and possibly dangerous for rescued survivors commuting from shelter homes. Regretfully (or should I say with great relief), we surrendered our deposit on the shack and began looking for other options.

Aloka came through for us, offering us the use of an outbuilding in her Child Care Home, a shelter at the edge of town. She identified twenty young women at the shelter who wanted to try their hand at metalsmithing. This seemed like the perfect place to start. We got a grant for the project and prepared, once again, to try something completely different.

37 ONE MILLION DOLLARS

Well, it wasn't actually a million dollars, but we did have a major reversal of fortune a few months later.

In April, our family drove from Florida to North Carolina, and spent a week checking out various places where we might relocate, or perhaps I should say re-relocate. Our first stop was St. Augustine, Florida. I had to give this quaint seaside town a serious look because John was still hoping we could stay in Florida. Though I liked it better than Palm City, St. Augustine still wasn't quite my cup of tea.

I tried to remain positive and open-minded, but I felt tense the entire time we were there. I was reluctant to remain in Florida after the past nine months of misery in the state.

Next we drove to Asheville, North Carolina, an artsy city in the Smoky Mountains, which has been called 'The Paris of the South' (or so they claim). Paris might be overstating the case, but nonetheless, I loved Asheville. I had been there several times years earlier, while on tour with my band. Asheville had grown a lot in the intervening twelve years, after being featured in many 'America's Best Cities' lists.

Unfortunately, John did not share the opinion of those magazines, or my enthusiasm for the city of Asheville. He was also concerned that the area, and North Carolina's state income tax, would be prohibitively expensive for us.

After a week on the road, the entire family was worn out and irritable. Esprit de corps was at an all-time low. The kids found it unsettling that we still had no idea where we were going to live, and that for the past nine months, we had failed to put down any roots. Clouded this family's future was.

Maya had a tearful meltdown in the car and begged us once again to move back to the Cape, even if just for one year. "I'm wasting my childhood, it's already almost over," she wailed.

Maya has a lot of stamina. A full hour later, I begged her to just stop talking about it, and we all went out for sushi, and in my case, generous lashings of hot sake. We opted to bail out of our reconnaissance mission a day early, so at 7:00 the next morning, we began the long drive home.

I was dejected, to say the least. I had held out such high hopes for us coming to consensus during this trip. I had hoped for us to find our hearts' new home, so we could begin enjoying the next phase of our lives. Instead, we were left with more doubts than ever, the kids were beginning to lose the plot, and I was having a crisis of faith.

'I'm wasting my life, and it's almost over!" I moaned silently, echoing Maya.

Everything seemed so uncertain. An expected grant renewal was many months behind schedule, with the amount still to be determined. Meanwhile, John was collecting unemployment, and our credit rating was heading south. That was not going to make it any easier to move because we would need good credit to rent a decent house.

Given my dark mood, perhaps it was for the best that John left as soon as we got home for a poker tournament in Tampa. This gave us each the opportunity to reflect in private on the decisions we faced. After eight days spent mostly in a car with my entire family, I was ready for some time alone. I let the kids watch hours of TV each day. They could have eaten entire bowls of sugar for all I cared.

I went for long walks, drank Chardonnay, and ate brownies with wild abandon. I started to feel the tiniest bit better. The kids watched the Disney channel and ate processed foods. They too seemed to find healing in these simple sacraments.

I came to accept that there was no perfect solution to the situation, and that was okay. I let go. I chose to stop agonizing and trying to find the perfect place to live. As I did so, I realized that we would all be just fine wherever we lived.

Because our first move had been painful and disappointing, I had built up a lot of anxiety around geography, rather than facing the decision with a sense of adventure and optimism.

By the end of the three day weekend, I was almost as good as new. I reconsidered St. Augustine, which I hadn't loved, but which, on further reflection, had real potential. It wasn't my dream town, but it was okay. And sometimes okay is just great.

Now that I was prepared to make my own luck and live with whatever came my way, the last thing I expected was a Hollywood ending. I was stupefied when John called to tell me he had just won $55,000 in the poker tournament! That is more than either of us earned in a year. It was a life-changing amount. In one moment, a year of debt and financial stress was erased. It made anything seem possible again. It was a miracle.

I'm not suggesting that everyone running a struggling business or nonprofit should expect to find their answers in legalized gambling. I've always encouraged John to treat poker as a recreational activity with no expectation of profit. We never expected to win such a huge amount, and likely won't do so again.

But on that one magical day, our worries were completely alleviated. Our future suddenly looked brighter and easier, with more possibilities and choices. Now we could afford to move, to replace our broken dishes, and to rent a nice house in St. Augustine.

God works in mysterious ways.

38   A CAN O' CALCUTTA

May, 2010:   I had made my peace with staying in the Sunshine State, but my daughter was feeling far from sunny.   Eleven years old and about to enter middle school, Maya now faced another move, to another town in Florida, and she was not feeling at all optimistic.   In fact, she was horrified by the decision.   I guess she was secretly hoping we would move back to Cape Cod in the end.

The situation brought home to me the fact that my children have made sacrifices for this work, as much as John or I.   Before I became a human rights activist, I was a full-time mom.   We lived in a spacious home that we owned.   We had security, and we had money for luxuries, like vacations, eating out, college...   Maya and Luke had witnessed, and to a small extent shared, the anxiety of trying to sell our house for two years.   They had to get used to a simpler lifestyle and more financial insecurity.   Then we had uprooted them and moved to a new town which they hated.   And now we were asking them to move again, to another unknown situation.

Luke took it all in stride, but Maya really struggled.   From the day in April when John won the poker tournament and we decided to move to St. Augustine, to the beginning of June when our bags were packed and ready, she cried every single night.   I was impressed by her stamina, but I felt like a heel for putting my child through such distress.

Up to a point.

And then, I reached the end of my rope.   I understood Maya was sad, and stressed, and eleven years old, and experiencing a flood of hormones, but enough was enough.   I used everything in my arsenal to help her put her troubles in perspective and cultivate a more positive outlook, but nothing worked for more than twenty-four hours. The following night she would work herself up all over again into a state of profound despair.

One night, with John out and Luke already asleep, Maya sat on the couch weeping as usual. I decided it was time for a different approach.

"Do you know *exactly* what I do?" I asked. She stopped sobbing and looked at me curiously. Of course, my kids had grown up with our work as a cornerstone of family life. When they were four, five and six, I explained it in terms of fighting poverty – helping poor children and their families. Once when Maya was five, I found her sitting on a blanket surrounded by small toys, neatly arranged in rows. "I'm selling these toys to help poor children," she explained in great seriousness. My heart sang. For a while, that was her favorite game.

When my kids were seven, eight, nine and ten, I went a step further and talked to them about modern day slavery and the work we did to fight it. There were stories in the books they read about historical slavery and child labor. Still it was hard for them, as it is for many adults, to accept that slavery and child labor still exist today.

However, I had never talked to my children about sex slavery. It seemed too brutal, too hard to comprehend. Sex itself is a strange concept for children. My kids had been appalled by the idea of sexual intercourse, even disbelieving, when I first explained it to them. The idea that it could be forced on children their age was too much information.

That night, I knew it was time to tell Maya the whole truth about my work. There are brochures and other materials all over the house explaining commercial sexual exploitation. It was only a matter of time before she read these for herself.

I explained the terrible things that were happening to girls her own age and even younger, and that it was so unbearable to me and her dad that we had turned our lives upside down to do something about it. I told her that most of the girls in my photos from India and Nepal - the girls she knew I loved and worked to protect - had been victims of sex slavery.

I assured her that she had every right to her own feelings, her own pain and human experience. I didn't want her to feel guilty for being sad.

God knows we all have our ups and downs! However, sometimes it helps to look at our experiences and feelings through a global lens – to put things into a larger perspective.

Yes, you can feel bad because you miss your friends and had to move to a town you hated, and now you have to move again and it's scary and lonely. Yes, I can feel bad because my husband didn't respond the way I needed when I was at such a low point, even after I moved to Florida for his sake. Yes, I can feel anxious because we're perpetually broke and never have enough help and there are hundreds of girls relying on me and it's a *lot* of pressure. Yes, you can feel bad because you lost your job, or you wish you were in a relationship, or you wanted to have children and it never happened, or your parents died, or your house is in foreclosure, or your husband just told you he's gay. These things really hurt, and we all have every right to feel our pain and acknowledge it and get help and support for it.

At the same time, it sometimes helps to remember that while we indeed suffer, others are suffering far worse. And we can share some of our energy, some of our time and effort and prayer and concern with those hurting people, even at our own lowest moments.

Maya cried some more when I told her about my other daughters, her sisters in India, Nepal, Cambodia and Thailand. These were silent tears, full of compassion. I could see that she was changed forever by this information.

After that night, Maya never cried again about moving to St. Augustine.

39 COMB THE SORROWS FROM MY HAIR

Later that summer, I joined Paul, the new 'Team India' and twelve volunteers for two weeks in Calcutta. This was the first time we had tried bringing volunteers in the summer, at the end of the monsoon season, when the city is miserably hot and humid.

We were in the final stages of separation from the Destiny Center at that time. The situation was still strained, and I was completely on edge. One day during the trip, I spent the morning in a tense meeting and then joined the volunteers at the Nijuloy shelter for the afternoon. I arrived at the shelter in an awful state. I was fuming, hurt, really quite beside myself.

We were painting a mural of ancient Egypt in the shelter's dining room. It was a steamy day, over 110 degrees, and rolling blackouts rendered the fans useless for much of the time. All afternoon I sweltered in the heat, meanwhile burning with indignation on the inside. Sweat stuck to the dirt and dust on my body, and I could feel it dripping down my back in nasty streams. Paint adhered to the sweat and splattered on my hair and nails. I looked a fright.

Hot as it was, one of the younger girls spent the entire afternoon plastered to my body, with her arms wrapped tightly around my waist. I tried to gently pry her off, so we could paint side by side instead of conjoined, but she wasn't having it. The darker side of my personality wanted to scream 'Please get off me! It's too hot to cuddle!', but of course I suppressed it.

I didn't think it was appropriate to share my problems with the volunteers. They had enough on their plates, with a hundred girls clambering for their attention, "Aunty, Aunty! Didi, Didi!" all day long, and an outbreak of dysentery at the shelter (less said the better about this).

I remembered how hard it had been for me when I first met girls recently rescued from brothels. The vicarious trauma is intense. The volunteers had their own complex emotions to cope with, so I suffered in silence. I became even more agitated because I couldn't talk my problems through with anyone. What had started as a relatively minor problem started to feel like a total crisis.

At 6:00, we finally stopped painting. I had been fantasizing for hours about getting back to my hotel for a cold shower and a warm beer (hard to get a cold one in Calcutta and I was in no mood to be picky). Most of all, I needed some time alone to indulge my bad mood. I couldn't wait to get back to my hotel.

Alas, this was not to be. Aloka showed up at the shelter in high spirits just as we were about to leave, and invited me and Paul to dinner at her social club. Since she had just driven several hours through rush hour traffic to pick us up, and was so excited to spend some time with us, I couldn't find it in my heart to refuse.

How could I possibly show up at a nice restaurant in the state I was in? I stood up, planning to wash up in the bathroom sink, but some girls forced me back down into the chair and surrounded me. They must have sensed I needed some loving care, because they spent the next half hour cleaning my hands and face with wet-wipes, brushing out my hair and gently scratching the paint off my hands and arms with their fingernails.

They refused to let me get up until they had finished the job. Someone found a clean tunic for me to wear, and a brightly colored scarf. By the time the girls finished, I looked quite presentable, and was in a much happier frame of mind.

This was one of the sweetest, most healing experiences of my life. It reminded me of a song I once wrote, called 'Comb the Sorrows from My Hair,' based on a painting of the same name by my friend Brookie. The song and painting celebrate the simple nurturing acts women perform for each other in times of need.

I was deeply touched by the girls' intuitive sense of my needs that day. Survivors have been betrayed so much in their lives, yet their generosity and kindness is so immense.

This work has never been a one-way street, with us giving the girls things and taking care of them. The success of this program relies equally on the survivors' own efforts. They have to take responsibility for their own lives and futures. We just provide opportunities where there were none before. For every inch of help we give the girls, they advance a mile.

And every chance they get, the survivors give the love right back to us.

40 PINKY

Looking at our school sponsored children, clean and well-nourished in their red school uniforms, I could hardly believe these were the same Kids we had met three years before in the Kidderpore red light area. Their ragged clothes and vaguely worried expressions were gone, but more significantly, the sense of imminent danger and vulnerability that used to surround them. Without it, some of the girls were barely recognizable.

"That's Tamanna?!" I asked in disbelief. "That's Monika? That can't be Kali!"

Our school sponsorship program is one of the parts of my work that I love best. Watching kids grow up safe and educated has got to be one of the greatest joys life can offer. I've observed through the years that educating a child through tenth grade practically guarantees she will not be trafficked, or re-trafficked into slavery.

When we first met the Kidderpore red light children on our earliest volunteer trips, most were not in school at all. I vowed at that time to do something for them. It took some time, but eventually my conviction evolved into a program.

The red light kids had difficulty attending local schools because of the stigma of being born into brothels. At first, we partnered with Apne Aap to send children who were coming to their drop-in center to a private school across town. There, the details of the children's background would remain private.

The children needed no coaching to avoid telling others about the fact that they live in a red light area. They have learned from a young age that they and their moms are considered pariahs by most people. The school administration knew only that our children came from deprived backgrounds.

Some of the smaller children acted out sexually when they first went to school, imitating behaviors they witnessed at home (for example, taking off their underwear or making suggestive comments or gestures). They soon learned how to behave appropriately at school and some became high achievers.

We found sponsors in America to pay for the kids' school fees and for van transportation to and from school. Apne Aap staff provided after-school support and tutoring. Mira and other community outreach workers went to the children's homes each morning to help them prepare for school, combing their hair, or waking them up in some cases. Mothers who had been working the streets all night were often too exhausted to get their children ready for school.

The program grew and expanded to include other shelter partners, Women's Interlink Foundation, Apple of God's Eye and others. By the end of 2010 we had 190 children sponsored for school.

After the first year of sponsoring the Kidderpore girls to attend private school, the staff at Apne Aap told us that some of the girls were no longer safe living at home with their mothers, or even in the night shelter. Some of these girls were in danger because they were reaching the age –eleven or twelve - where they might appear to be 'fair game' by clients. Others were at high risk because their mothers were physically ill, neglectful, or absent from the scene.

Sahana, a member of the Apne Aap staff, worked tirelessly to secure placement for ten girls at Ram Krishna Mission, a prestigious boarding school three hours outside Calcutta.

When the children were living at home, they shared a tiny room in the brothel with their mothers. This is a dangerous situation because there is always the risk that a client will tire of the mother and reach for her young daughter instead.

The red light area is a scary place for a child to grow up. There is never enough food, clothing or attention and the kids have to become self-sufficient at a very early age. Seeing their mothers hurt and exploited on a nightly basis is agonizing for them. Without intervention, girls growing up in red light area almost always end up in forced prostitution themselves.

In August, I went with Sahana to visit the children at the boarding school. It was a paradise. Gardens of vibrant flowers and huge trees flourished all over the campus. Groups of children in tidy uniforms ran and played in safety in the large gated campus. The children were receiving a top quality education and were now able to communicate with us in English.

The most dramatic change was in their personalities. Kali, who was depressed and severely underweight before, could not stop smiling for the whole two hours of our visit. She is still willowy but healthy, whereas before she was so thin, we worried she would not survive to adulthood.

All of the children were more confident and hopeful than before. They shared their plans to become doctors, teachers, police officers and social workers. Most of them want to do something to improve the lives of people in the red light area when they grow up, or to punish traffickers and free their mothers. These futures are now a realistic possibility for them. With an education from Ram Krishna mission, they will be able to go to college and become professionals.

Spending time with Pinky was especially poignant. Pinky, who I introduced earlier, is an exceptional child. She is academically gifted and a natural leader. She's tiny and feisty and I have always adored her.

Pinky's mother had died just two months earlier from tuberculosis, a common problem in the red light community. Pinky's mom was one of the sweetest ladies I have ever met. Unlike some of the other mothers in prostitution, she never neglected or abused her child. She was tiny and full of love, just like her daughter.

When Sahana mentioned Pinky's mother, Pinky burst into tears. I held her on my lap and cried with her. I promised to always be there for her, and to mother her as best I could. Love was all I had to offer in this tragic situation. For the thousandth time, I hoped it would be enough.

41 THE TOUCHABLES

After the volunteer trip, Paul and I traveled to Varanasi with one remaining volunteer, Tanja, to visit villages recently freed from slavery. One of these villages, Firojpur, was the site of our newest school sponsorship program. We called it the Freedom School.

We had been invited by Bhanuja Sharan (bonn-ōō-jah shā-ronn), the Director of MSEMVS. This is the agency which the volunteers were unable to visit on the first ill-fated Varanasi/Bihar trip. Since then, we had begun partnering with MSEMVS to support a three-year project to free and empower the village of Firojpur.

We took an overnight train from Calcutta to Varanasi. The trip took fifteen hours. We had sleeper berths, but I slept fitfully because roaches were crawling all over my face and body. It wasn't scores of roaches, just two or three every hour or so, but normally I would be having a nervous breakdown if even this small number of roaches were crawling on my face. This was just one of those times along this journey, where I was able to completely let go. For some reason, I found the grace to accept something really revolting and not freak about it.

We spent two days with MSEMVS, visiting eight villages within a four hour radius of Varanasi. Since there were no bathrooms in these villages, and nary a tree to squat behind, we deliberately dehydrated ourselves so wouldn't have to use the bathroom during the ten-hour journey. That was uncomfortable, but given the circumstances these people faced, it would have been obnoxious to complain.

The families in these villages were all members of the Dalit caste (aka 'untouchables'). They had been enslaved for three generations to pay off small debts incurred by their parents or grandparents.

Some of the villages we visited had been freed only a year before, others as long as seven years previously. The difference was dramatic.

The people of the first village we visited had been free for only a few months. Sitting in a circle with the women of this village, listening to Bhanuja explain their situation, I was suddenly overwhelmed with sadness. I was surprised when tears began to well up in my eyes. This was totally inappropriate! Nobody wants to be an object of pity, and the predominant mood of the meeting was one of hope.

I struggled to get my emotions under control. This reaction was out of character for me. I see and hear about so many tragic situations, I've trained myself to repress my sadness until I can process it in private.

For some reason, the courage and stoicism of this particular group of survivors broke through my defenses. Perhaps it was the fact that many of these women were my own age, yet their life experience has been so different. All the years I spent going to college, traveling, building a career in music, getting married, buying a house, having children, launching a nonprofit, these ladies were toiling in a brick kiln or quarry. They spent a lifetime being powerless and hungry, under constant threat of physical or sexual violence. While I was sending my kids off to preschool or soccer, they sent their children to stack bricks or break rocks. It was brutally unfair.

Because the project in that first village was so new, many of the children showed signs of malnutrition (red, fuzzy hair is one of the signs, along with distended bellies). Still, their happiness at being free to learn and play for the first time in their lives was apparent. You could see in some of their faces that they didn't quite believe that their luck would hold.

In the village square, I sat on the ground swapping songs with members of a women's self-help group. Theirs was a low, haunting melody which was sung by one group of three women, then echoed by another trio, back and forth across the circle. Paul and I busted out an energetic but raspy version of 'You are My Sunshine'. Our voices were ragged from dust and dehydration, but no one seemed to mind.

I tried to get the women to stop fanning me with giant banana leaves, as it made me feel like a pampered eighteenth century British noblewoman, but my face was bright red and there were flies all over me. The women felt sorry for me and chose to ignore my protests.

Despite the flies and heat and lack of bathroom facilities, the gift of this day was to live fully in the moment. It was a once-in-a-lifetime opportunity to share the unbounded joy and appreciation of people recently freed from slavery.

It was terribly hot and dry, but the countryside was green, beautiful and peaceful. It was a welcome respite from two weeks in a city of twenty million. The women's bright saris made a stunning contrast against the background of mud and brick houses, brown earth, and green fields of rice.

Although we could only communicate through a translator, I enjoyed sitting with the women, sharing smiles, and hearing their dreams and plans for the future.

"You are a woman, so you will understand," said one lady. "We just want the best for our children: to go to school rather than to work. And for ourselves, we want only the chance to choose our work, and to be paid for it, to care for our families and to help others. I hope you will support us".

Women who had been rescued from slavery were now advocating for the freedom of their neighbors in the surrounding villages. Their bravery and compassion was extraordinary. I felt humbled by their example.

In another village, the women told us that when they refused to work as slaves, the 'powerful people' destroyed their road to the outside world, in an effort to isolate and frighten them back into submission. For two years, the villagers petitioned the district government to build a new road, travelling for five hours by tractor, bicycle, and on foot to make their case with district authorities. One community member died in the process. Finally, the villagers prevailed, and they now have a fine new stretch of road connecting them to the rest of the world.

I asked them what challenges they still face. "Without challenge, there is no life," one woman replied. "There will always be troubles and challenges, as long as we are alive in this world. But as long as we have our freedom, we are ready to take them all on".

We purchased thousands of handmade glass beads from the village women's groups. These would later be made into earrings and necklaces by the survivors at our jewelry center in Calcutta.

Paul described the day perfectly in his Facebook post later that night:

"Hot and humid, flies on face, no food or bathrooms, five villages freed from slavery, best day ever!"

The next day, we drove three hours from Varanasi to visit our Made by Survivors Freedom School. MSEMVS had begun an intervention in the village of Firojpur in 2009, and enlisted us, through our friends at Free the Slaves, to sponsor the Freedom School. The first step in the process of freeing a village is to convince parents to allow their children to attend school rather than to work.

My heart sang when I saw the simple thatched-roof school, and the fifty-two children, aged four to twelve, who were learning there. Just one year ago, these little ones were working alongside their parents in stone quarries or on farms. They had either never been to school, or had been forced to leave school to work with their families. Despite their lack of educational background, the children were quickly catching up. The older ones had advanced in just one year from kindergarten to third or fourth grade level.

When people are literate, they can know their rights and read a contract. Education helps to ensure they will never be tricked into slavery.

One of the greatest benefits of the Freedom School and the whole MSEMVS outreach program is how it has united the community. Before MSEMVS came to Firojpur, every family stayed in their own hut, isolated, ashamed and afraid. This fear-based social system ensured that no one ever fought back against the slaveholders. The enslaved Dalits had little contact with each other, and their only contact with the outside world was with the people exploiting them.

Again, we sat with the women of the village, and asked about their dreams and struggles. The Firojpur women told us they were putting forward a candidate for village headman (mayor). Dalit people in this region have never had a political voice, let alone held office, so this would be a huge breakthrough. We found out later that their candidate Rekha won the election, changing the course of history in this one village.

Our final stop was at a brand new project, in a village which we were the first Westerners to visit. The arrival of three tall, yellow-haired Americans caused quite a stir. We felt like celebrities as the entire village of two hundred gathered to greet us.

I could visit another thousand villages before I found a community of people so grateful for their freedom. As little as these people had, they felt rich with freedom and opportunity.

When it was time to leave, the entire village insisted on walking with us to our car. I felt so blessed to be walking among them, not in front, nor behind, but all together, united in purpose.

When we reached the car, one of the women timidly asked if she could shake our hands. To us, this was an unremarkable way to conclude a meeting with new friends. But for the Dalit, who have grown up being told they were untouchable, to shake the hand of someone you have just met is remarkable indeed. We ended up shaking the hands of every man, woman and child in the village. Many people began weeping openly. This time I let my own tears flow as well.

Many of the women took my hand and placed it on their foreheads – a gesture representing the desire to absorb someone's wisdom and experience. I put their hands to my forehead too. I have so much to learn from their courage, and their wisdom won through brutal experience. They have seen the worst that life has to offer but have not been broken by it. They know what really matters, and nothing and no one will stop them from fighting for it.

They are free.

42   LIVIN' THE BRAND

August, 2010, Boisar, India - three hours outside Mumbai:

Paul's normally calm and cheerful demeanor was stretched to the breaking point. "Oh no, these cannot be maggots in my #@$%& shoes!" he moaned. But yes, they were maggots. He stomped back to the truck in utter disgust. It's hard to stomp when you're squelching barefoot through mud, but somehow Paul managed to do so.

The Calcutta jewelry program had been running for four months, and already we could see success and enormous potential. The survivors loved forming beautiful objects out of slabs of hard metal. It was a powerful metaphor for the transformation they were experiencing in their own lives.

Using the tools, and power tools especially, was empowering for them. Receiving a regular paycheck, and bonuses for exceptional work and productivity, was more empowering still. Every single girl in the jewelry program had grown self-esteem and in the ability to imagine a future for herself.

Imagining the future is a bad idea when you are living in a brothel. It's better to zone out and get through each night moment to moment. The less present you are, the better. When girls are rescued, they often retain this survival skill of detachment for many years, or forever.

"What are your dreams for the future?" I asked Sonali in the early days of her training.

"I don't have any dreams, only nightmares," she said, looking away. *Best not to pursue that discussion further*, I decided.

Three months later, Doel asked Sonali the same question. "I plan to become an expert jeweler and manage this program," she replied. "Oh, and I also want to set up a program like this for poor women in my home village". Sonali wasn't alone in her desire to give back. Most of the girls in the program expressed the ambition to become trainers and program managers as well as master jewelers.

Encouraged by the progress in the survivors' lives, we decided to expand the jewelry program to Mumbai. We hoped to partner with Rescue Foundation, and outstanding organization that I had first visited in 2008.

Rescue Foundation is India's largest trafficking rescue organization, pulling hundreds of girls out of slavery every year. They use a system of in-brothel counseling followed by rescue raids. Rescue Foundation receives leads on missing girls from agencies such as Maiti Nepal and Sanlaap. Or sometimes, members of the red light community act as informers when very young girls are brought into a brothel.

Upon receiving a lead, Rescue Foundation starts an investigation, and sends an undercover investigator to the brothel where they have heard reports of trafficking or underage girls. An investigator begins visiting the brothel and buying time with one of the girls. He begins a long process of in-brothel counseling, gaining the girl's trust so that when the time comes for a raid, she does not just run away and hide.

This is necessary because the girls are brainwashed by the traffickers to believe that anyone claiming to want to help them will only hurt them worse, or even kill them. They are afraid of the police because of police corruption. Some policemen turn a blind eye to child prostitution in exchange for free services at the brothel.

Women and girls in prostitution are treated so disrespectfully by clients, neighbors and passers-by, they come to believe that they are no longer fit for normal society. They believe what they are told by everyone they see: that they are irreversibly ruined and worthless for anything but commercial sex.

An investigator will spend weeks or months building a relationship of trust with one or two girls in a brothel. These girls then spread the word to the others that a raid is coming and that the rescuers are the good guys.

In-brothel counseling is incredibly dangerous for the investigators. If they are caught, they risk being badly beaten or even killed. Their only protection is to fly under the radar as much as possible.

Once a girl is adequately prepared, Rescue Foundation makes arrangements with a few trusted police officers to conduct the raid. They inform the police at the last possible moment, because there is so much corruption in the force. Too many times in the past, when the police knew about the raid in advance, someone alerted the brothel keepers and the brothel was cleared out by the time the rescuers arrived.

When the raid occurs, the brothel owners try to hide the girls, underground, behind false walls, or even rolled into carpets. Some girls run away or claim they are over eighteen and that they are in the brothel by their own choice, even when that is not the case. The devil they know is less terrifying to them than the unknown.

Others risk everything in a daring bid for freedom, running out to meet the rescuers, telling the rescuers where other girls are being hidden.

When I first visited Rescue Foundation with Becky, it was to attend a wedding of four survivors. These young women dreamed of living in a village, getting married and starting their own families. They thought it was an unattainable dream, since their own families and villages had rejected them, blaming them for what was done to them.

Triveni Acharya, (trih-vēn-ee uh-chā-ree-ah) the Director of Rescue Foundation, refused to accept this. She went to her home village and found young men in their late twenties who were unable to find girls to marry because there are more young men than women in India. This is the result of years of selective abortion and female infanticide.

One progressively-minded young man was willing to be the first in the village to marry one of Triveni's survivors. He was adamant that she be accepted into his family and community.

People in the village saw the couple's happiness, and got to know the young bride, and soon other young men became willing to marry survivors. In this way, one community was transformed from within, to become more humanistic and accepting. Rather than judging the survivors as bad girls and attaching shame to them, the villagers now understand that trafficking survivors are victims of a social evil.

The wedding that Becky and I attended was a celebration of life that I will never forget. Hundreds of girls from Rescue Foundation's three shelters were in attendance. Hand-painted signs, streamers, and silk curtains transformed the shelter's dining hall into a temple and banquet hall. The ceremony went on for four hours. People came in and out, chatted and snacked, while the priests and families conducted a complex ceremony involving fire and spices and scarves and prayers on a raised stage.

When the ceremony finally concluded, we all enjoyed a feast. Then it was time to say goodbye to the brides, who had been living at the shelter for several years. Triveni gathered all her girls in a large circle, and they began to hug and weep. Becky and I joined the circle, hugging and crying too. After about ten minutes, we stepped away. Ten minutes is already more than the prescribed amount of crying for a wedding in our culture, and we didn't wish to intrude.

Forty-five minutes later, Triveni and her girls were still wailing, still saying their heartfelt goodbyes. Fast forward two hours: they were still crying with as much emotion and energy as ever! Finally, three hours after the beginning of the long farewell, the brides got into a bus with their new husbands and families and drove away.

The next morning, I came to understand the advantage of this lengthy public outpouring of emotion. I asked a few young girls if they missed their sisters who had gotten married the previous day. They looked baffled.

"Miss her? Why would I miss her? I'm happy for her, she wanted to get married". They had no need to be forlorn. They had fully expressed their loss the previous day. Now they were free to get on their lives, rather than silently moping for days, which is what I would have done.

Ever since the wedding, we had been looking for a way to partner with Rescue Foundation. Paul and I flew to Mumbai from Varanasi to meet with Triveni to discuss the possibility of opening a jewelry center at her shelter outside Mumbai.

We found Mumbai refreshingly cool and rainy after our sojourn in a near-desert climate. August is the tail end of monsoon season which begins in May. Early in the monsoons, rain can fall so hard and fast the streets flood up to your knees with water and sewage runoff. People literally dance in the streets because the rain is such a relief after the intense heat of spring.

We met Triveni and her right-hand man Mahesh at their office in the shelter home. Like most shelters for rescued survivors, Rescue Foundation was protected by an armed guard. Unlike most others, their guard carried a machine gun. There had been more than one incident of traffickers attacking staff members' cars, trying to break into the complex and causing an awful ruckus.

We had prepared a slide presentation about our jewelry program to show Triveni. The first slide pictured a group shot of twelve of our survivor-jewelers in the doorway of the Calcutta jewelry workshop.

Triveni crowed with surprise and delight "Wait…that's Sonali! That's Monu! That's… another girl I can't remember her name but… those are all girls we rescued and sent back to West Bengal. I can't believe they're in your program!" This was a most fortunate coincidence because it made us feel like we were already working together. We were already one big happy family, with daughters in common. It gave Triveni confidence to see girls she had rescued glowing with happiness, and to hear how much they were earning in our jewelry program.

We later discovered that the girls in the picture, after being rescued by Triveni's team, had been sent to Sanlaap shelter in Calcutta, and eventually transferred to Womens Interlink Foundation, where they joined our project.

Triveni agreed to partner with us and let us set up a center at her Boisar (boy-sāhr) shelter three hours outside Mumbai. The next day, we drove from Mumbai to the Boisar shelter with Triveni and Mahesh.

In the year since Becky and I had visited, we had raised funds to build a bio-diesel facility at Boisar shelter. The bio-diesel facility provided renewable energy for cooking gas and hot water heating. Bio-diesel is a fuel created from cow dung, so there were now forty cattle living on the shelter's farm. The cattle provided not only dung for fuel but also fresh milk for the survivors.

Triveni was excited to show us the cattle shed and bio-diesel system. It was still raining hard, so the farmyard was a giant puddle of mud and dung and monsoon rainwater. I was, for once, wearing the proper footwear (this time, it *was* flip-flops) but Paul was not so lucky in his canvas sneakers. Sadly, when he took his soaking, dung-covered sneakers off, they were full of maggots. Yuck! This was almost as bad as the lice I brought home from my next trip to Boisar, but perhaps it's best we not go there…

One of the girls rushed to rinse Paul's feet with water from the well, but he was past help. That was when he stomp-sloshed back to the truck.

Back at our hotel later that night, the whole incident seemed more hilarious than foul, especially since the day had ended on a high note, with a formal agreement for us to open a new jewelry center at Rescue Foundation.

Paul is always talking about 'living the brand'. When he worked at The Body Shop, this meant using the company's toiletry products, and sharing their values of concern for animals, indigenous cultures, and the environment.

Now, 'living the brand' meant working long hours for a quarter of the salary he used to earn, overwhelming challenges, flies on his face, (or worse, roaches!) and sharing his shoes with maggots.

It also meant sharing the joy of freedom with people who never dreamed they could be so happy. Living the brand doesn't get any better than this.

43 CULTURE SHOCK

"You are looking very fat, Sarah," said Debjani, smiling warmly. *Did she Really just say that?* Exhausted, dusty and ragged-edged after a hard week in Calcutta, I was in no mood to be insulted. My face must have betrayed my dismay, because Debjani hurried to reassure me. "I mean, you are looking very good... *and* fat. But it looks very good on you!"

Saying a woman is fat is not a big deal in India, the way it would be in America. No matter how chubby a friend or relative has become, only the most insensitive American woman would ever remark on it.

In my defense, I wasn't any fatter than usual when Debjani made this comment, which is in my opinion, not fat at all, maybe just a little curvier than the modern American ideal. Nonetheless, my Indian friends have seen fit to remark, on many occasions, that by their standards I am fat, or that other volunteers or staff members are fat.

In South Asian culture, the word 'fat' just doesn't carry the same heavy (pardon the pun) burden that it carries in Western culture, where an extremely high value is placed on thinness. In India, no one really cares how fat or thin you are. Most people there are slim. It's hardly a selling point. It could even mean you are poor and hungry.   In India, your weight is just like any other attribute – height, hair color, language – that can be used to describe you, and it's fair game to comment upon without any need for delicacy.

With close friends, like Smarita, I have had to make a rule that comments on my weight are off limits. I know it sounds shallow, but I just can't cope with people telling me I'm fat every time they see me. Even though I understand that this is a cultural difference, I can't help feeling offended when someone mentions my weight, and then I have to spend the next five days nervously checking my appearance in every mirror, window or reflecting pool. I thought I was evolved enough, and had a body image positive enough, not to care. Come to learn I'm not and I don't, just one more hard truth this work has taught me about myself.

While the issue of how fat or not fat I am is hardly significant, we have had to figure out some more relevant cultural differences to keep this cross-cultural enterprise from getting lost in translation.

1) The Asian 'No' (aka 'Day After Tomorrow'): In the American business world, we put a premium on directness, punctuality and frank honesty (remember when I said John was blunt to the point of rudeness when he first joined the team?) In South Asian business, politeness, relationship-building and not disappointing a client are more highly valued. We didn't understand at first that these two sets of values can be incompatible.

In one instance, we placed an order of bags from a partner in Nepal. We needed the bags in two months, and said so at the time we placed the order. The partner agreed. 'No problem, Acha, Acha' (Good, good). When the deadline arrived, we contacted the partner, asking if the order was ready to ship. "Day After Tomorrow," they told us breezily. It was Monday, so we assumed that meant the order would ship on Wednesday. A week later, the shipment still hadn't arrived, so we emailed the partner. It turned out the shipment still hadn't left the workshop in Nepal. "Day after tomorrow," they promised again. The process was repeated.

Finally we figured out that 'Day after tomorrow' was not a phrase denoting a specific time frame. It was an expression which really meant 'I like you and care about your business so I don't want to disappoint you. Therefore I won't say "No, your products are not ready'.

The same phenomenon occurred when we asked a partner agency to do something they didn't want to do, or weren't comfortable with. Instead of saying 'No', which might hurt our feelings or seem rude, they would nod or give a non-committal head bobble (could mean Yes or No) and then the idea just wouldn't happen. 'No' is not something you say to people you like and respect, so the Asian 'No', to the uninitiated, looks more like 'Yes'. Confusing, right?

2) Chain of command: Another cultural nuance which we had to learn how to navigate was the chain of command. Asian companies tend to be more formal and hierarchical than American ones. At first, we didn't understand this, so we would often make the mistake of discussing plans with lower level program staff members at our partner shelters before discussing them with the upper management.

The program staff members were our friends who took care of us when we visited the shelters, and who went out to dinner with us in the evenings. It seemed natural to bounce ideas off of them. However, they weren't the ones with the power to make decisions. We later learned it was considered rude to discuss plans and ideas with them, even in a casual way, without first asking their bosses. Everything had to go through the proper chain of command. On several occasions, I have had to write letters apologizing for gaffes related to this cultural difference.

3. Color and Design. South Asian art and fashion is some of the most exuberantly colorful on planet earth. Even in the poorest villages, women till the fields in beautiful saris in a rainbow of gorgeous colors, embellished with gold thread. Holidays are a feast for the eyes. Temples are ablaze with color. The love of color is one of the things I love most about India and Nepal.

However, when it came time for the Indian and Nepali survivors to design and create products for the Western market, their color aesthetic didn't always work. The more colors in a piece, the better: that seemed to be their motto. Why use just one color when you can use five!? More's the merrier. Red with yellow, red with green, why not? 'Because we only use those colors together for Christmas', I explained. Turquoise and fuchsia and chartreuse and orange, there truly seemed to be no limit.

We lost a lot of money in the early days on products that we couldn't possibly sell. We came up with the idea of sending designers and design and business professors to teach our artisans about Western design tastes and entrepreneurship. These instructors help our artisans to develop their own design vision, and to find design inspiration in their experiences and the world around them. Then, with a knowledge of both local and international tastes, they can apply their designs to create products for either local or international customers.

For all the cultural differences we've had to navigate, I've learned that humility and a willingness to admit when you get it wrong, are the fastest routes to repairing a bruised relationship. Working together, with a lot of tolerance and love, and with some coaching from our own Indian staff members, we're figuring it out.

'I'm sorry, I was wrong' have become five of the most powerful words in my business vocabulary. That's a case where cultural differences work in my favor, because admitting you are wrong in such blunt terms is unusual in Asia, so when I say it, people appreciate it.

When Paul first moved to Calcutta, he cut his hand and had to go to a clinic for stitches. After stitching and bandaging his hand, the doctor gave him some supplies to keep the wound clean, and sent him on his way with the encouraging words, "Don't worry. The Spirit will protect you".

Paul smiled politely, but made a rueful face as he walked away. He's a logical and pragmatic person and he found it odd for a medical professional to make such an overtly religious comment. Patients should not be relying on supernatural protection, they should get proper medical treatment, he thought.

Later, when Paul told me the story, I hooted with laughter. "She didn't mean 'the Spirit will protect you'. She meant 'the spirit will protect you', as in 'mineral spirits', the Indian term for rubbing alcohol". Still chortling, I pointed out the label reading 'mineral spirits', on the bottle the doctor had handed Paul on his way out of her office.

44 HOW DO YOU DO IT?

One question I am often asked is "How do you do it? How can you be involved in such a depressing, appalling issue?"

I can't emphasize enough the value of life's simple pleasures in helping me cope with the anguish of this issue. Wine, chocolate, tea, exercise, singing, watching movies with my family, playing with my dogs, and going out with friends are my personal favorite ways to unwind. I need to include as least one or two of those every day to maintain my positive attitude (and it can't always just be wine and chocolate). When things get really crazy at work, I usually slip and lose all sense of balance. Then I start feeling exhausted and hopeless, and have to recommit to self-care.

Another thing that helps me stay positive is the camaraderie of the people on my team. Made By Survivors has always been a team effort, and our esprit de corps has helped me through many tough times.

Launching the jewelry centers was a challenge for everyone on the team. On the U.S. side, we had to reinvent our marketing, to shift our customers' mindset from buying funky, ethnic handbags for $10 each to sterling silver necklaces costing $50 or more. We also needed to find new ways of telling our story and the girls' stories as the scope of our programs expanded from human trafficking to other human rights issues.

Many of the women making our products are survivors of different kinds of abuses, not just trafficking and slavery. Some were forced into child marriages. Some grew up in prison or on the streets because there were no orphanages willing to take them. Some were born into red light areas, and at high risk. Some were raped during wartime. All are survivors of one kind or another, and deserve help to reach their limitless human potential.

When Dianna first started the jewelry training, she said it was hands-down the hardest thing she had ever tried to do in her life. The first group of trainees in Calcutta included twenty young women. Many were traumatized. All had extremely low self-esteem. Twenty students is a large number for one jewelry trainer under the best of circumstances (which these weren't!).

Our space was small and we had to get creative, training the girls in shifts, and having half the group practice or draw in another room when they weren't on shift.

In the first few months, there were tearful breakdowns at jewelry class every single day. Metalwork is frustrating and hard to learn. Saw blades break. Filing and sanding take forever. You can easily make one wrong move and ruin a piece you have spent hours creating.

The girls' lack of confidence, added another level of difficulty. Dianna also observed the effect of extreme trauma on the girls' short term memory. She would have to repeat the same instructions over and over again, even for the brightest girls who had no problem absorbing harder concepts. This memory problem wasn't an issue for the high risk girls, only the recently rescued survivors. It seems that extreme trauma can actually change neural pathways, and reduce brain function. Over time, the benefits of creative self-expression and working in a loving, safe environment helped to reverse the damage, and the girls' memory improved.

We also struggled to find tools that could be purchased locally (we carried over all our tools in overloaded suitcases until finally locating a source in Mumbai), and to find precious metals. We were dismayed to discover when put our first jewelry collection online, that it was in fact *not* sterling silver and our supplier had been ripping us off for months.

We lost trainees from the program due to personal problems, girls being repatriated, girls running away, as well as the fact that metalsmithing just isn't for everyone.

What kept us all excited and positive that first year was the growth we witnessed in the survivors as their skills increased, and the exuberant joy that filled the workshop more and more each day. We came to know and love them as little sisters and daughters. Each one has such an incredible story.

A few lucky girls, like Angura, mastered the skills of jewelry making quickly. Angura had an innate artistry which we first noticed when we were painting a mural at her shelter home. Angura is profoundly deaf and was abandoned by her parents. Little is known about her childhood, and she came to Women's Interlink Foundation as a teenager. She had never learned sign language or been around other deaf people, nor was she able to communicate verbally.

Angura refused to live in a world of isolation, so she created her own means of communication. She and a twelve-year-old friend at the shelter developed their own sign language. With the twelve-year-old acting as translator, Angura was able to communicate quite complex concepts. When she found out we were starting a jewelry program at the shelter, she insisted on being included in it.

You would have thought Angura had won the lottery when we invited her to join the program. No one in any of our programs, before or since, has picked up skills faster than Angura, despite her limitations in communication. Friends from the local deaf charity Shaktura have since come to teach Angura and our staff some Indian Sign Language to make communication easier.

Another survivor named Sweety had one of the toughest stories I have ever heard. At the age of five, Sweety witnessed her father murdering her mother. Her father was sent to jail, and because there was no orphanage available to take Sweety, she was sent to grow up in a women's prison. She grew up there from age five to age twelve, until Aloka found out about the situation and rescued her. Not surprisingly, Sweety was traumatized from years of neglect in such a violent, chaotic environment. She had spent much of her childhood chained to the floor.

After two years at Nijuloy shelter, receiving loving care, Sweety began to recover. She became able to control her explosive rages and to interact normally with other children. Then, inexplicably, the Child Welfare

Council made the decision to move Sweety to another shelter home. Aloka fought the decision in court but lost, and Sweety was taken away to a government shelter home, where she was neglected and surrounded by deeply disturbed children. By the time Aloka managed to get her back a year later, Sweety was in such distress, she was psychotic, babbling incomprehensibly, and striking out at the slightest provocation.

A few more years of loving care restored Sweety once again to sanity, but when we met her at age nineteen, the years of pain were etched on her face in a permanently distrustful scowl. When Dianna stood behind her to teach a technique, Sweety would flinch from the touch. Eye contact was out of the question. She never smiled or laughed with the others.

Sweety didn't have Angura's innate artistic ability, so it took longer for her to master metalsmithing. However, her gift was a dogged determination, and she persevered as her skills developed, slowly but surely. Today she is one of the team leaders and a very able artisan.

A year into the program, Sweety married a local boy and had a baby. Her love of jewelry, and of her husband and child, has transformed not only her personality but her very appearance. Her face now glows with hope. There is a softness in her features that was not there before. She is her family's highest earner.

Priyanka's story is perhaps the most inspiring of all. Priyanka grew up at the shelter for many years because her mother, a brothel worker, didn't want her anywhere near the red light district. Like many of the mothers in prostitution, Priyanka's mom believed that Women's Interlink Foundation could provide her child with a better home, education and healthcare. Most importantly, growing up in the shelter provided Priyanka with the opportunity to break the vicious cycle of children who are born into brothels becoming brothel workers themselves.

Priyanka was one of the first girls to join our jewelry program, and to be honest, she was no great shakes at first. She paid little attention to Dianna's lessons, talked and distracted others during class, and sometimes failed to show up on time, or at all. Sometimes, she came with a negative attitude, but mostly she just seemed disinterested.

Thankfully, a month into the program, Priyanka realized she loved working at the jewelry center and decided to stick with it. The improvement in her work ethic was immediate and obvious after she made the decision to apply herself. She began showing up on time and worked hard throughout the day. She stopped complaining about things she couldn't control. Instead she focused on improving the things she could. What a fine example for all of us! Priyanka eventually became one of our strongest jewelers, and designed some beautiful pieces that we added to our first collection.

Meanwhile, Priyanka's mother, who was still living in a brothel, was no longer able to earn money due to her age. Like all the older women who have spent their lives in prostitution, Priyanka's mom had developed serious health problems. She felt trapped in the red light district, but had nowhere else to go. She began to despair of the future, and feared that she would end up dying alone on the pavement outside a brothel, despised and abandoned.

Priyanka went to visit her mother in the red light area, and saw that something had to be done. She loved her mother too much to see her in such dire straits. She realized that she was empowered to help, and made the decision to get her mother out of the red light district once and for all.

After earning and saving for a year in the jewelry program, Priyanka saved enough money to rent a small apartment for herself and her mother, far from the red light area. Priyanka now earns a sufficient income to provide for all of her and her mother's needs. She is overjoyed to be able to live independently for the first time in her life, and also to be able to pull her mom out of the hell of the red light area.

Paul rejoiced in his blog: "This is a HUGE victory for all of us …. A young woman feels empowered enough (and has the resources to back it up) to move out of the comfort zone of her shelter home and into a new place to help take care of her ailing mother. And she did this, not because she found a guy and got married to him (the usual way shelter home girls get out on their own) but because she learned a skill and used it to build a better life for herself and her family".

These heroic young women, the victories we get to witness, and the support and friendship we give each other: *that* is how we do it.

45 ALL MY CHILDREN

Like every woman, I've played many roles in my life: daughter, sister, friend, wife, artist, employee, boss, activist, hellraiser, unpaid cleaning lady and many more. But the one role that has given me the most joy and satisfaction is being a mother.

John and I always planned to have a large family, with two biological and at least two adopted children. Shortly after Luke's first birthday, we began the process to adopt our third baby. We settled on China as the country of origin, chose an agency in Boston, and began the extensive application process.

As it happened, our first home study interview fell on the day after my mother's cancer diagnosis, so we had to cancel. During the three months of Freedom's illness, and the year after her death, I was much too upset and overwhelmed to think about adding another child to our family, so our adoption plans had to be put on hold.

Then I saw the film which turned our lives upside down, and we spent the next six years crafting a program to fight slavery. This exhausted our personal and financial resources. We were too busy to do anything else, and could no longer afford $25,000 or more for an international adoption.

Then, in late 2010, our circumstances changed radically once again. My stepmother Ann died of cancer, leaving me an unexpected inheritance. Ann and my dad had worked hard and invested wisely. They saved money for a long and comfortable retirement, but since both died in their early sixties, they were able to leave a staggering $200,000 to each of their four children.

When Ann's illness began progressing rapidly, she told me how much money she was leaving us. I was speechless. My dad and Ann had always told us 'we're going to leave a little something for each of you guys,' but this was far beyond what anyone would call 'a little something'. It was enough to buy a house.

After selling our house on Cape Cod, we never expected to buy our own home again. Our salaries, when we could take them, were just enough for our monthly expenses, and we had no money saved for a down-payment. I had accepted the fact that we would likely be renting for the rest of our lives, and that was fine.

Still, buying a house could reduce our stress, and give us a greater sense of financial security. The kids were thrilled with the idea of owning our own home again. They were very aware of the financial insecurity we had been living with. They wanted the family to choose a permanent home and stay in it. With inheritance from my parents, we bought a house in St. Augustine, in the same neighborhood where we had been renting. Every day in my new home, I think of my sweet dad and stepmother, and give thanks for their generous bequest which made it possible for us to live here.

After putting a down payment on the house, paying off debts, and putting some money aside for emergencies, we still had $25,000 left - enough to pay for an international adoption.

Our work, though still busy, had become better organized and more mature. I was now in a place where I could consider parenting another child, and there was nothing I wanted more.

With Maya and Luke in fourth and sixth grade, and John and I in our forties, we decided against adopting an infant. We now aimed to adopt a child between four and eight years old, who would still be the baby of our family, but not so far in age from his/her older brother and sister. Ethiopia had one of the fastest and least expensive adoption programs, and it resonated with all of us.

Once again, we collected all our paperwork, filled out reams of forms, and sent off large checks to the adoption agency. Maya and I spent many happy evenings that winter poring over the impossibly cute pictures of Ethiopian kids on the adoption websites.

In the middle of all this family excitement, in early 2011, I went again to India. This visit proved to be one of the busiest and richest to date. We had a great group of volunteers that year, and were also filming a short documentary about our work. For the purpose of filming, I visited each and every one of our projects and Calcutta and Mumbai, and even some sites where we weren't running projects ourselves, but were supporting partner agencies' efforts, like the Sonagachi red light district. Sonagachi is the feeder district for girls at Nijuloy shelter (one of Aloka's shelter homes where we had been sponsoring kids and painting murals for years, and where many of our jewelry center girls resided).

Sonagachi is Calcutta's largest red light area, a huge warren of narrow lanes with a population of 25,000. We went at night to visit the children in Aloka's red light night school, including girls who would likely end up at Nijuloy in the coming months and years. Most of the mothers give up their daughters willingly to Aloka, knowing that their future in the red light area holds nothing good.

As always, the drop-in center was an oasis in a sea of human misery, the lanes where row upon row of girls lined up, blank-faced and blessedly absent from their own bodies. I had mastered the skill of neither looking at the girls nor turning away from them – a non-intrusive, compassionate witnessing. Covertly, I plotted escapes for each of them.

Inside the center, we were deluged by little children. There were thirty kids and two teachers in a space the size of my bathroom. Space in the red light districts is expensive and hard to come by. I made myself as small as possible (quite a feat because I'm a statuesque woman) and was soon enveloped covered head to toe in three and four year olds.

One girl in particular captured my heart. She had huge eyes which she kept trained on me for the entire forty minutes of my visit. She was unusually calm and focused, and like all of the children, absolutely beautiful and precious.

The second center we visited was larger. It served as a schoolhouse for fifty elementary aged children. "Look closely at that wall," the teacher suggested. I realized the walls of the room were actually the exterior walls of adjacent buildings! The floor underneath our feet was cobblestone street. With no space available to rent, Aloka and her staff had simply put a roof over the street between two buildings, slapped on some large metal doors, and called it a schoolhouse.

My visits to the boarding school sponsored kids, the jewelry centers, and the other shelters where we worked were equally inspiring. Everywhere I went, I saw happy, well-educated children and empowered young adults. I felt pride and deep satisfaction knowing that I had contributed something to their happiness and success. These were all my children.

I spent my final day in Calcuttta with Aloka at the Nijuloy shelter. We talked about the little ones in Sonagachi. We spent some time comforting two little girls who had just arrived at the shelter from Sonagachi and were homesick and missing their mother. I put a few finishing touches on a mural we had painted that week, but the survivors at Nijuloy were mural veterans by that point. I had to concede I was becoming obsolete when it came to muralizing.

Near the end of the day, I asked Aloka what help she needed over the coming year. She thought for a moment, and then pointed to the larger of the two buildings at the shelter, which housed vocational training programs, a dining room and kitchen.

"That building was always intended to be two stories high" she told me. "If you could possibly raise some money to build the second floor, I could take in another twenty-five girls from Sonagachi."

My mind flashed back to my tiny friend with the big eyes at the Sonagachi night school. She and the other girls in those centers would be the very ones who could live in safety if that floor was built.

"How much would that cost?" I asked.

"Mmmmm… about twenty five thousand dollars"

I think we all know how this story is going to end.

We had $25,000 with which we planned to adopt one child. Or, we could use our $25,000 to welcome twenty-five girls a year into our extended family. Our family could provide a safe, happy childhood to hundreds of girls over the course of the building's life. These would be girls who are already in a program we support, and we will surely come to know and love them all in the years to come.

Later, when I talked to John about my change of heart, he shared my desire to build the shelter with the rest of our inheritance, rather than moving forward with the adoption. We were already blessed with two children, plus five hundred. And we had long ago chosen to cast our lot with *these* children - former slaves and kids born into brothels in India, Nepal, Cambodia and Thailand.

Hey Sandy, we're not poor, we're rich in children!

46 JOHN'S RULES

We all have personal rules that we live by and force those we love to live by. Mine are that no one can eat standing up around me (it makes me feel rushed and tense). Also, I don't like to be asked questions with an obvious answer, like "Where do you keep your cheese?" (in the fridge, of course! In the *cheese drawer* in my fridge). Thirdly, I have certain words which I simply cannot tolerate, such as dramaturge (it means someone who edits plays, but please don't let's discuss it further).

I can not and will not discuss work or anything else until I've had my first cup of tea in the morning. And that tea must never, ever be made with water heated in the microwave. That's disgusting. My dad once made tea for me that way and claimed it tasted just the same as properly boiled tea. It did not. The poor guy's been dead for six years and I still haven't gotten over it.

John has five hard and fast rules in his work life, which have profoundly impacted the way we do things. His first rule is that you can't talk about serious matters right before bedtime. It could make you tense and disrupt your sleep, plus it is sure to put the kibosh on any intimate relations.

Second, you must <u>never</u> say you feel overwhelmed. I was a little chagrined when I first heard this rule because I used to love saying how overwhelmed I felt. I found relief in admitting it, and it made me feel virtuous in a pleasantly martyrish way. And I was, in fact, frequently overwhelmed in the early days, trying to fight global slavery while raising preschoolers, with no staff or budget, and with programs and expenses that just kept growing, no matter how hard we tried to slow them down.

John insists that saying you are overwhelmed is counterproductive.

Announcing and giving attention to it just makes you feel more overwhelmed, admitting defeat and announcing to the world that you are powerless. Thanks to John, I never say I feel overwhelmed anymore. I simply do as much as I can do each day (and sometimes a little more after that) and accept that I will never get to the bottom of my to-do list until I die, and in this I am no different from any woman I know.

Another one of John's rules is that you must never say '*I'm doing the best I can!*' He feels it's a form of whining. It's also a cop-out. You might in fact be able to do better. You could approach your problem from a different angle and might get better results. Just 'doing the best you can' is not going to help anyone if the ultimate outcome is poor. Survivors don't need us to do the best we can. They need us to shut up and keep trying until we succeed.

John's fourth rule is that you should never start a new program just because you can get funding for it. Starting new programs should be based exclusively on the needs of your population and your organization. Further to that, you should never start a program – even if you do need it – with no funding (although this is a rule we have been obliged to break rather often).

John's fifth and most beloved rule is that you have to be willing to fail – again and again – in order to have an epic success or do something groundbreaking. '*If you aren't failing, you aren't taking enough risks,*' that's his motto. If you aren't taking risks, you won't succeed in business, and business is the tool we have chosen to help our survivors.

Although I have been blessed with success and good fortune in many of my efforts, we've also had a large number of failures and setbacks. So here is an abridged, and by no means comprehensive list of things that I have tried and failed at:

- Running large-scale awareness campaigns about slavery

- Creating pink survivor-made products for breast cancer

- Home parties, after the first two years (tried and failed repeatedly to do this)

- Running a school sponsorship program in Uganda (ended up getting entangled in an international bank fraud)

- Being a shopkeeper

- Raising lots of money (have yet to master this important skill)

- Selling watches, embroidered pants (yikes), bags made from garbage, tank tops and many more products which utterfly flopped.

- Employing people who were already my personal friends

- Most of 2009

- Giving up sweets or wine for more than a week at a time. (I did manage to stop biting my nails when I began traveling to Asia, but now I simply pick at my nails with my other nails so I'm not sure it really counts as quitting)

These are only a few highlights of my many missteps and failures. But the good news, the really *great* news, is that we are still here, still moving forward, and sevearl thousand women and children have a better life as a result.

On my first trip to Nepal, I heard the Nepali folk saying 'The elephant marches on, heedless of the barking dogs'. It means that no matter what anyone says, and regardless of the negative voices, even the ones in your own head, despite the disappointments, lost opportunities, struggles and failures, you just keep marching on. And that's the best rule of all.

So bark away, dogs! I haven't got time to listen. I have to go help my sisters rebuild their lives.

47 RAISE THE ROOF

After the usual growing pains, our jewelry center in Mumbai began to thrive. Dianna spent six months in 2011 training survivors in Mumbai, and developing higher level skills in the Calcutta team.

It wasn't easy. In Mumbai, she lived at the shelter home, eating spicy curries three meals a day, struggling to make herself understood, waging a daily battle against head lice and dysentery, and counseling (with her limited language skills), extremely traumatized girls , some of whom had been rescued as recently as six months earlier.

Few staff members spoke English. Internet and cellphone coverage was spotty in the remote area where the shelter was located, and Dianna was frequently lonely and homesick for her new husband Jeff. They had been married only a few weeks when she left for India. The whole situation would have been unmanagable if it weren't for the courage and creative genius and utter awesomeness of the survivors.

Kiya from Nepal speaks five languages. Her parents sent her to a monastery school because members of her extended family were involved in human trafficking. Her parents were too poor to provide for her and feared for her safety. Regardless, when Kiya was in her early teens, she was drugged, kidnapped and trafficked from the school in Nepal to a brothel in Mumbai by her aunt who is the brothel owner. As it turned out, this aunt was the very person Kiya's parents were trying to protect her from.

After a year or two in the brothel (girls tend to lose track of time once they are living in a brothel), Kiya was rescued in a raid conducted by Rescue Foundation in conjunction with local police.

At the time we started the Mumbai jewelry center, Kiya was sixteen years old and a star student. She also excelled in athletics, especially karate, and she soon became one of the leading artisans in the jewelry program. Despite the pain of her situation and feeling betrayed by her family, Kiya soon distinguished herself as a leader in the group of twenty-five trainees.

Baby is one of the most talented designers we have ever had in our programs. She was twenty-three when she joined our program. Baby was born in Bangladesh into a very poor family, and was put into a child marriage at around age twelve. Child marriage is a common way for parents in South Asia to cope with extreme destitution, and to secure a future for their daughters. Although Baby was very young, she tried hard to make her marriage work, and eventually gave birth to a daughter.

Unfortunately, she was trafficked to Mumbai at age eighteen, by persons unknown. In the course of being trafficked, Baby jumped from a moving truck in an escape attempt, and broke her leg in the process. The traffickers threw her back into the truck, and the injury was never treated, so she now walks with a limp.

At the time we started the Mumbai program, Baby had not seen her daughter, now age six, for several years. Thankfully, Baby's daughter was safe, living with her sister in Bangladesh. Through her income from the jewelry program, Baby was soon able to support her daughter, and to pay for the child's education.

Baby advanced quickly in our program due to her innate artistic ability, emotional maturity and motivation. After six months, Dianna promoted her to team captain. Baby amazed us all with her prolific designing. We added many of her jewelry pieces to our collection.

When we first started the program in Mumbai, repatriating survivors from India to Bangladesh was a lengthy and difficult process. The Bangladesh government did not want the girls back, and resisted every effort to send them home. Baby and many others had been stuck in India for years, waiting for their legal status as Bangladeshi citizens to be proved so they could return home.

Baby was torn between a desire to return home to her daughter and sister (her husband refused to speak to her after she was rescued) and her wish to keep earning and developing her skills as a goldsmith.

One day when we were visiting the center, Baby approached John and our Board Chair, Elizabeth Goldberg.

"I am feeling torn about whether I should push to return to Bangladesh, or keep quiet and stay here longer," she told them. "So... I need you to open a center like this in Bangladesh, and I will run it for you".

Who could say no to such an offer? Not us. No mother should have to choose between supporting her child and being with her child, especially after being forced apart for so many years by trafficking. We began brainstorming about how to open a center in Bangladesh for Baby to run.

One of the frustrations of operating our program at the Boisar shelter was that the jewelry program was housed in the same large bungalow that housed the shelter dining hall, the school, and other job training programs like hairdressing and tailoring. The situation was chaotic to say the least.

Rescue Foundation asked for our help to construct a new building for the school and vocational programs, including the jewelry program. We raised about $50,000, and Rescue Foundation raised funds from other donors. By March, 2011, they had four walls and and a floor constructed but the building still lacked a roof. The monsoon season was perilously close.

I reached out to my friend Kathleen McGowan, a bestselling author who had come into my life a few years earlier. Kathleen's writing and life mission centers on the subject of the divine feminine. She reached out to her large community of readers for help raising the roof at Boisar shelter. She set a goal of raising five thousand dollars for the project. Within days, her friends and fans had contributed over ten thousand, and the roof was built, giving over a hundred survivors a place to learn and heal. Of course, we later added a mural to the space!

48 WHAT ABOUT THE BOYS?

Ajay was fifteen when he came to Calcutta to take a six month carpentry course at Apne Aap. When the course ended, Ajay refused to return home. "If I go back home, I will be forced to sell my own sister and mother," he stated bluntly. "I will sleep on this agency's doorstep if I have to. But I won't go back there".

Ajay comes from a region in Bihar where intergenerational slavery has been practiced for hundreds of years. In the nineteenth century, his community, the Nutt, served as courtesans and circus performers. Today they struggle with desperate poverty, trafficking, and crime. Almost every girl in the community is trafficked into prostitution at a young age.

Having seen another way of life in Calcutta, Ajay knew he could no longer bear this injustice, or worse, be forced to play a part in it. He was given temporary housing in Apne Aap's office and drop in center, and eventually got a job there as a security guard.

Ajay's refusal to perpetuate the cycle of slavery and abuse illustrates one of the problems facing boys in impoverished and red light communites. Without intervention, they too are at risk - the risk of being forced to become traffickers themselves.

Boys worldwide are also victims of trafficking and slavery. They are equally at risk as girls for being trafficked for labor or begging. They are at higher risk for being trafficked as child soldiers or camel jockeys. In certain industries, such as carpet loom weaving, boys have traditionally been the ones targeted for exploitation. And in some parts of the world, young boys are trafficked for sexual exploitation, although in the areas we work, it is predominantly girls who are used for this kind of slavery.

So much of my journey and work has centered on girls – girls who have survived slavery, girls growing up in the red light areas or border towns, girls denied education or basic human rights. However, I have come to appreciate how important it is not to neglect the boys in any situation.

If we fail to address the needs of tomorrow's men, and to teach them to respect and value women, we will forever be putting a band-aid on an open wound, rather than preventing that wound from occurring in the first place. We need to teach our sons about women's rights. We need to talk truthfully and frankly with teenage boys about prostitution, trafficking, pornography, and how these things are connected.

The boys in our program are as sweet and heroic as the girls. Many, like Ajay, have suffered from seeing their mothers and sisters trafficked and abused. These boys are loving and protective by nature. Whenever we need to visit a red light area at night, our boys are close at hand, a pack of small but fierce bodyguards.

On one occasion, Becky was working in Kidderpore in the evening. The boys suggested she should head home to avoid any problems walking to the bus stop. The route to the main road wound through three long lanes of brothels, where men are often violent and drunk. The boys offered to be Becky's bodyguard and walk her to the bus stop. Five young boys flanked her, one holding each hand, two in front leading the way, and one behind her. As they walked, men made rude comments but the boys just kept their eyes straight ahead, occasionally pausing to tell the men to show some respect.

Like Made By Survivors, our partner Apple of God's Eye in Nepal used to work with just girl survivors. The girls in their home came to Silvio and Rose one day a few years ago, to talk about their brothers, who were still either out on the street or living in destitute villages where trafficking is endemic.

"You are taking such good care of us, and we very, very grateful" the girls said. "But how can we be completely happy when we know our brothers are not happy or safe? Is there any way you can help our brothers? If there is not enough food, we will get by on half as much. If there are not enough beds, we can sleep on the floor! Just please do something for our brothers!"

In the face of such selfless concern, Silvio and Rose could not refuse. They found a way to begin bringing the girls' brothers into the home, and now operate two homes for boys as well as four for girls.

Like their sisters, many of these boys are now committing their lives to social service. The older boys who grew up in the program provide security for the female survivors when they conduct prevention programs in dangerous border villages.

We can't move forward as half a people. We need brothers and fathers as well as sisters and mothers in this cause. I can't imagine our organization without all the loving, powerful men who are part of it – John and Paul, McDonagh and Dan, Chan and Mahesh and Bhanuja and so many others.

The boys in our program have the potential to transform their families and communities. They can protect and advocate for women rather than exploiting them. They can become businessmen, doctors, policemen, or social workers and loving fathers, rather than traffickers or brothel clients. Just like our girls, they need help and support to overcome the obstacles in their lives and reach their highest potential.

It's so simple. For a vulnerable boy or girl, all it takes is for one person to intervene, for one person to refuse to accept the status quo. Any one of us can make the difference between poverty or slavery and a happy, successful future for a child. We each have the power to be a one-man or one-woman Underground Railroad.

49 SOW THE WIND, REAP THE WHIRLWIND

Diary Entry, April, 2012: *Something incredible is happening this month in Jalpaiguri, something we have dreamed of, and planned for, and talked about for a very long time. Our survivors are traveling from one city to another as the trainers and mentors for our new jewelry center in Jalpaiguri.*

These women stopped being victims a long time ago, becoming survivors. They took the opportunities they were offered, and grew into artisans and entrepreneurs. Now they are becoming activists – leaders of a new generation of empowered women. I'm so proud I can barely stand it!

Our Calcutta jewelry center was thriving, and the women were earning more than their families and peers, more than their husbands, more than they themselves had ever imagined. Seeing this success, Aloka asked us to launch a third jewelry center in the remote region of Jalpaiguri, near Darjeeling. She has a shelter home in that region, and there is a desperate need up there for economic opportunities.

I thought it over for about five seconds, and then said "Yes!" John as usual, was more circumspect. He ran the numbers, analyzed the feasibility of adding a new center, created budgets and spreadsheets, and asked our Board of Directors and staff for their input.

Thankfully, since I had already impulsively said yes, we were ultimately on the same page about the project. It was a go. However, we still needed to come up with some money. We applied for, and got, a few grants, and I set up a campaign on our website to raise the rest.

We were going to need a fair amount of money because it turned out there was as yet no shelter building up in Jalpaiguri. Instead, Aloka was housing the survivors in a rented house, not nearly large enough for the number of girls needing shelter. We agreed to help construct the shelter in addition to starting a training and production center in Jalpaiguri. I fretted (uselessly, as fretting always is) about how we were going to raise that kind of money.

In August, we received some sad news. An old friend of ours from John's investment banking days, Naved Khan, had died suddenly at the age of thirty-eight from a heart attack. Naved was a loyal friend and long-time supporter of our work. I was surprised, and deeply touched, when his wife Helena reached out to us just a month after his death. She felt inspired to get involved with Made By Survivors, continuing the work that Naved had begun. By the end of 2011, through Helena's fundraising efforts, and the generosity of many donors, we had raised enough money to launch the new jewelry center, and some of the money needed to build the new shelter.

In the past, I had only ever thought about Darjeeling in the context of my morning tea. I imagined a misty, mountainous area, lush with tea bushes, relatively unpopulated, a paradise. In reality, the region is indeed beautiful, misty and mountainous, but it's also rife with poverty and human rights emergencies, including human trafficking.

In early 2012, we launched a jewelry program in the rented shelter space. This program was a real breakthrough for us because it was the first time that our survivors, trained in the Calcutta program, would be doing much of the training for the new girls. They are fantastic role models for the new girls because they come from the same background. They know what it feels like to grow up in a shelter home, to come from a red light area, to be impoverished or to survive slavery. They understand the wounds those things leave behind, and how those wounds can eventually heal.

Often when the girls are training, they have a crisis of confidence, and break down in tears. Their self-esteem has been destroyed by dehumanizing treatment and a lifetime of being undervalued.

"You just don't get it, you can't understand. I can't do this!" one girl cried in frustration during the first month of training. She threw down her tools and burying her head in her hands.

"Actually, I do get it," said Sunny. "I grew up in a shelter home too, and I cried a lot when I started learning jewelry, because no one ever thought I was good at anything, and I didn't believe I could be good at anything either. But now I manage a whole jewelry center of twenty girls. I traveled here alone on a train for the first time in my life, and I'm staying in a hotel for the first time in my life to come here and train you girls. So stop crying and let's drill this pendant!"

My goal, and John's, from the very beginning has been to make ourselves redundant. We have endeavored to give the girls every tool they need to manage all aspects of this business and charity. I'm feeling pretty good about how we're doing with this goal.

I know that in the future, the survivors who grew up in this program, or who have found healing here, will not just be executing my vision. They will be creating their own projects and healing the world in ways I have never even imagined. Some are already doing so.

These girls, or their children, will end slavery once and for all. They will help to create a world that is safer and more equal for women and girls.

Sow the wind, reap the whirlwind.

50 SMALL THINGS

<u>True Confession of the Day</u>: I spend a lot of time worrying that we're not doing enough. I worry that our organization is too small, that we're not helping enough people, and that we should somehow be much further along by this point.

I'm committed to making a significant, long-term difference in survivors' lives, rather than helping a larger number of people just a little bit. However, I still sometimes look at other charities with huge staffs and million-dollar grants and tens of thousands of people in their programs, and feel slightly inadequate.

Whenever I start to indulge these unproductive thoughts, the survivors' stories get me back on track.

Puja is one of the girls in the jewelry program. She's eighteen years old, 4'10" tall, and almost painfully cute. When our jewelry program in Mumbai first began, Puja became very close with Dianna. She would patiently, relentlessly talk to Dianna for hours, using the few Bangla words that Dianna understood.

Puja would say 'chota' all the time, which means small. She said it about what what she was making, about herself, about little children and flowers. 'Kitna chota hay?!' 'Chota, chota.' 'Mai Choti hu, Ap bari hay'. (How small this is?! Small, small. I am small, you are big). She was desperate to communicate, even if it required her to talk like a preschooler to teach Dianna Bangla.

Puja is dedicated and very able. She quickly began picking up English. She grew into one of our most accomplished jewelers. She has an impeccable moral compass and refused to get caught up in any teenage drama at the shelter.

When Puja was little, she lived with her family under a tarp in a Calcutta slum. Her parents sent her to the train station to look for work when she was ten, and a few years later she was trafficked out of the train station to a brothel in Mumbai.

After a short time, Puja managed to escape through a barred window in the bathroom. Incredibly, she found a police officer and bravely returned to the brothel to rescue three of her friends. She later testified against her trafficker, which is very unusual.

Puja had been training in the jewelry program for a year when she received her orders from the Indian Court system to be transferred from Rescue Foundation to a shelter home in her native Calcutta. The goal was for her to be reunited with her family. Puja was desperate to see her mother and father again, so we were happy for her, although sorry to lose her from the program.

We worried about whether we would ever see Puja again after her transfer, if she would be able to find work and earn money safely, and to which shelter home she would be sent. We found out she was slated to be sent to a shelter outside our network, and it seemed like it was a done deal.

Dianna was adamant that Puja should be transferred instead to Women's Interlink Foundation shelter. That way, she could continue to pursue her career as a jeweler, and would be able to see our staff members, who she knew and loved, every single day.

Paul and Dianna decided to ask Aloka if Puja could be transferred to one of her shelters in Calcutta. They knew it might not be possible, because there might not be space, and because Aloka had never worked with Rescue Foundation before.

Security needs to be tight at the shelter home. A cell phone snuck in from the outside world can compromise the safety of over a hundred girls. Traffickers camp out all day in empty buildings near the shelter and throw cell phones and notes to the girls inside, trying to trick them into running away.

Paul and Dianna met Aloka for dinner to discuss the situation. Dianna was on tenterhooks, desperate to find a safe haven for Puja. She launched into a lengthy monologue about Puja and how special she is and her tragic story, hoping that Aloka would consider the transfer.

When Dianna paused for breath, Aloka smiled gaily and threw open her arms. "Well, my dear, why don't you just transfer her to me!"

Aloka helped facilitate the complex repatriation process. She told Dianna and Paul she would be happy to take in any of our girls from the Mumbai program who were transferred to Calcutta.

Dianna then contacted Triveni, President of Rescue Foundation, who agreed to petition the court for Puja to be transferred to Women's Interlink Foundation. Triveni agreed that it was in Puja's best interest to stay with people she loved and trusted, in a stable and well-paying career.

We felt proud that our relationship of trust with these two exceptional organizations helped to forge a new partnership between them. In South Asia, relationships are everything. It can be downright nepotistic in fact, but in this case, it worked in our favor.

Dianna wrote in her blog:

'Not only did love and teamwork keep Puja under our wing, but, it laid the groundwork for more transfers which will keep talent in our jewelry program and allow the survivors to earn good money… Their ability to work helps to ensure their continued success, and ultimately, freedom in life'.

Puja is now happy and secure, living and working in Calcutta, thanks to Dianna's love and persistence on her behalf. Sadly, when Puja first got back to Calcutta, she learned that her father had died while she was trafficked. The news was devastating, but thankfully she had the support and love of our staff and the other survivors to help her through the loss. She has made a strong recovery and is now a leader and a hero in our program.

Puja is just one tiny young woman, one survivor from a poor family. She is a small thing in the eyes of many. Sometimes people are more impressed by large-scale programs and numbers than by one life changed forever.

I struggle too with this crazy reasoning. I sometimes feel disappointed with what we've achieved in comparison to the high expectations I had in the first few years.

I've learned that changing big problems takes time, and unbelievable perseverance. Our organization is employing hundreds of survivors, not ten thousand. We are educating a few hundred more. Our buildings and other projects shelter and nurture another thousand or so. Let's face it, these are not Nobel Prize-winning results.

However, I'm pretty sure God does not care how many people any of us help. All that matters is that we do our best to help each other through.

If I have saved even one person, if I have given even one girl the tools to build a beautiful life out of the ashes, then that small thing is worth everything. If I asked Puja, I bet she would say it was worth it.

51 HOME

What is home? Is it the place where you keep your stuff, where you live permanently, where your mail gets delivered? Is home the place where 'when you have to go there, they have to go take you in?' (Robert Frost)

On the visit to India and Nepal in the spring of 2013, I was as completely at home as I have ever been in my life. Home is where people I love jump for joy when they see me. Home is where I can express all aspects of myself, where nobody expects me to be Saint Sarah or super-efficient Sarah, or to be good at accounting or writing HTML. I'm just Sarah Aunty, who keeps coming back because she loves us, and that's enough.

Home is our 'house that love built', the programs where I see the fruit of my labors in the happy lives of women and children. Home is the feeling of contentment and emotional honesty that I don't get anywhere else.

I began with a visit to our newest project in Jalpaiguri, near Darjeeling in the northeast of India. I was joined by my friends Kathleen (who helped raise the roof for the Mumbai shelter) and Susan Shaw, a design professor from Falmouth University in the UK.   The new shelter at Jalpaiguri hadn't been constructed yet. We were still raising funds for it, so in the meantime thirty-two survivors were housed in a small rented apartment as a short-term measure.

Most of these girls had been rescued very recently from human trafficking, severe forms of child labor (like sweeping the floors of trains or picking tea on a plantation, while also being sold for sex), or they are at high risk because their mothers, aunts, and sisters are in prostitution.

A few streets over, another rented space houses our jewelry training program and overflow dorm rooms.

For the past eighteen months, I had been running a fundraising campaign to build a permanent shelter home for these girls and a hundred more. The need is immense. Jalpaiguri is near the borders of India, Nepal, Bangladesh and Bhutan. Just being so close to these borders puts girls at higher risk for trafficking.

The region's economy once relied heavily on tea farming, but many of the big plantations have closed over the past decade, plunging an already poor economy into real crisis. Girls are being trafficked to brothels from the tea plantations and from impoverished villages. Many are members of tribal or low caste communities. Despite the dire trafficking problem, Women's Interlink Foundation operates the only shelter home in the district for rescued survivors of trafficking.

Before visiting the girls in the rented shelter, we went with Aloka to see the land where the new shelter is to be constructed. It was a lovely, peaceful plot of green in the countryside, a few miles outside of town. The shelter's driver, Bolla, had originally put a down payment on the plot to build a home for his own family. When he learned that Aloka needed land for the new shelter, he generously transferred his claim to her. Bolla came with us to view the land, smiling proudly as we admired it.

"So let's speak frankly," I asked Aloka as we stood on the land. "How much money do we still need to get this shelter built?" We had all hoped that other sources of funding could be found to supplement the $60,000 I had raised the previous year, but so far no one had stepped forward. Jalpaiguri had no champions yet, apart from us.

"We had to use some of your donation to fix up the rental space," said Aloka, "so we still need another $50,000 to build the ground floor of the new home… but it's going to be really large and beautiful when it's done".

I indulged a brief moment of despair. How was I going to raise another $50,000? It had been hard enough to raise the first $60,000, and I didn't feel optimistic about going back to the same community of donors with the same need a year later.

"I'll help you raise that money," Kathleen said quietly. "and we'll do it in six months. I can ask my readers and friends. I'm sure they will help us. It *has* to be done, so we'll just get it done".

"When do you need the money by?" we asked Aloka. It felt good to have someone else standing up for our girls. I no longer have to embody all the optimism and energy we need to do this work. I have a team of people alongside me now who share my belief that these girls have suffered enough, that they deserve to be happy and safe and rich in opportunity. I was flush with gratitude and relief as we got back in the car and drove to the rented shelter home.

Many of the girls at Jalpaiguri had been rescued very recently, and were markedly more traumatized than our girls in Calcutta and Mumbai. One was unable to speak at all about her trauma, or about anything else. She had been brought in by the police the previous month and had not spoken a word to anyone since. Did she even understand Bangla? She could have been a member of a tribal language group. Or was she just too upset to speak? No one knew.

Another girl, Richa, began to cry when Aloka asked whether she might like to try the jewelry program. She just stood there silently, tears flowing down her face, unable to reply. In the brothel, it is a necessary survival mechanism to live moment to moment and not to think about the future.

Richa had long since given up hoping that she could have options for her life, outside of being sold and used night after night. To suddenly have a range of options was so far beyond her experience and expectations, it was overwhelming. Richa was sixteen but looked about thirteen, my daughter Maya's age. I wanted to fold her in my arms and cry it out together, but we had only just met, so I held back.

The girls in the jewelry center had been waiting for us all day. It was after 5:00 by the time we arrived and the sun was just beginning to set. A giant flower and the word 'Wel-come' were drawn in marigold petals at the entrance of the center. When we walked in, all the girls cheered and we felt like celebrities. Then they turned on the overhead fan and showered us with flower petals they had hidden on the fan blades! It was magical.

Over the next three days, we got to know the girls as we assisted Susan, in leading a series of design workshops. Susan created these workshops to be a condensed version of the same university-level design instruction she gives her students in England.

Our girls lit up as they discovered newfound talents, design inspirations, and ways of seeing the world around them through Susan's workshop. Meanwhile, we sat among the girls, holding their hands, pouring love into them with all our might. They were hungry for love and attention, more as much as any group I ever worked with.

Their stories, we soon learned, were also more horrific than usual. Nina spent her childhood working at a roadside hotel with her mother, washing dishes and being sold for sex. Sweet and quiet Sanjana was tortured by her family after she ran away with a boy from another caste.

"I won't tell you what they did to her, because you would never be able to get it out of your mind," said Aparna, our Program Director at Jalpaiguri. "Suffice it to say you would never be able to believe that someone could do that to their own sister or child".

Anika's brother-in-law sold her, along with her infant daughter, to a circus and traveling brothel so he could steal her small inheritance. She was enslaved there for years, doing whatever it took to survive and to keep her young child from being exploited. She was used so badly during that time that she went through eleven forced abortions.

Anika's daughter Anala, now eight, lives with her mother at the shelter. Anala has the sunny personality and breezy confidence of a child who has never been exploited. Anika paid the price for that child's easy smile with her own body and soul.

When we first arrived, Anika wore a perpetual frown and seemed alienated from the other girls. When we saved her a seat next to ours, she looked surprised and fearful, but came cautiously to join us.

We were stunned two days later when Anika stood up and read aloud her team's presentation on consumer branding. It turns out Anika has a high school diploma and is extremely intelligent. She possesses education and sophistication far beyond that of the other girls, but most of the time remains locked inside her painful memories.

"What is your dream for the future?" we asked Anika after we had gotten to know her.

"All I want is to care for my daughter, and wander freely," she answered.

To support our children, to have the freedom to live and travel where we want: these are dreams common to all mothers. We vowed to do our best to help Anika achieve them.

When it came time to say goodbye, the girls were taking their midday nap. The dorm was hot and crowded, with two and three girls to a bed, and some sleeping on mats in the hallway. This overcrowding leads to the fast spread of illnesses. There have been outbreaks of typhoid, dysentery, chicken pox and flu after flu over the past year. One girl had to be moved out of the shelter because she had tuberculosis, an unacceptable risk in this close environment.

As we hugged the girls goodbye, and promised to return as soon as we could, we renewed our vows to build a safe and permanent home for them. It was the least we could offer these girls we had grown to love.

Later that week, we were describing our Jalpaiguri trip to someone outside our organization. We tried to explain how we had come to love the Jalpaiguri girls so deeply in such a short time. "But how can you love them? You've only known them for three days," the woman asked skeptically.

Here is my answer for that question, variations of which I get asked quite regularly: Love is not a feeling, it is a commitment. While feelings ebb and flow over time, the commitment to love someone is forever.

When I decide to take a group of girls into our program, I make a commitment to love and support them for the long term. I know from experience that these relationships will only get deeper and better with time, and that our team will be there for the girls, loving them and working to improve their lives any way we can.

I know that a powerful love and mutual respect will grow as we nurture the girls' dreams, so why deny myself the joy of jumping in and getting started right away?

We flew back to Calcutta, where we met up with John, and with Tiffany Weston, a three-time India volunteer and loyal friend. Tiffany is a person who always has exactly what you need – lip gloss, a mint, Dramamine, a tissue, a vacuum-packed hiking bag filled with fine wine – and gives it to you before you even realize you needed it. That's why we call her 'The Tiffany of Requirement'.

The four of us spent the next few days in Calcutta with Paul and the rest of our India team, doing workshops with our kids in the shelters and slums. As usual, it was exhilarating, heartbreaking, and exhausting.

Tiffany and I cried during a special ceremony to inaugurate the new floor at Nijuloy shelter (the one built with our adoption money, along with donations from Tiffany and one other donor). We lit candles with Aloka to bless the new building. We walked through it hand in hand with the girls and listened as they shared their dreams for the future.

I can't think of anything more precious than a child's dream for the future, especially when that child has already been to hell and back and still has the faith to dream at all. When we first started, I listened to the kids' dreams with equal parts hope and fear. I feared that the brutal circumstances of their lives would crush their dreams before they could be realized. I worried that I didn't have the power or resources to stop this from happening.

Now I felt nothing but gladness, knowing that for these children, anything is possible. And for any part I have been able to play in securing their bright futures, I am ridiculously, indescribably grateful.

52   FINDING GRACE

As I've mentioned, I've always wanted more children.   To be absolutely accurate, it's not just that I wanted more children, it's that I've always known I was *going* to have more children, or that I was *supposed* to have more children.   I'm greedy that way.   I love being a mom, and obviously my work reflects that.

In March, 2013, I found my daughter Grace, or to be completely accurate, we found each other for the second time, and adopted each other as mother and daughter.

I first met Grace at Sanlaap shelter in 2009, just weeks after she was rescued, along with twenty-four other Tamang girls.   These were the girls who balked at our paper bag puppet project, because scissors and glue and tiny pom-poms were so far removed from the life they had been living in the brothels, or in their destitute villages.

Grace had been trafficked to India not once but two times, with a rescue and a brief stint back home in between.   She became vulnerable when her father, the village schoolteacher, died.   Her mother became severely depressed and unable to protect her daughter.

After a year recovering at Sanlaap, Grace and the other Tamang girls at Sanlaap were repatriated back to Nepal.   I never knew that she and several of the others ended up at our partner agency Apple of God's Eye.

Last Thanksgiving, our friends Silvio and Rose, who run Apple of God's Eye, visited our home in Florida.   Silvio was flipping through some pictures on his laptop when a picture of Grace and another girl popped up on the screen.   'That's Grace and Marcia,' Silvio pointed out, scrolling rapidly on to the next photo.

"Wait, can I see that one again?!   Is that Grace Tamang?   Was she at

Sanlaap before she came to you?" Yes, it *was* my Grace. I ran and found the card she had decorated with leaves and left for me on our last day at Sanlaap.

When you meet a girl soon after rescue, a very special bond is possible. Trafficked girls have been betrayed so completely, they have to start all over with loving and trusting. In this way, they are like small children, and it is impossible not to love them fiercely.

It takes patience and extreme gentleness and restraint to break through the barriers that recent survivors have built around themselves. When it works, and you are able to forge a relationship, you are intensely grateful for the honor that has been bestowed on you – being one of the first, or sometimes the very first person that a survivor chooses to trust.

I have had that honor a few times, and I'm not exaggerating when I say I would lay down my life for the girls who have given it to me. Every time it happens, it breaks my heart and changes me forever.

In Grace's case, the strong feelings of attachment I felt for her were equalled by her own, and undimmed by the three years between our first and second meetings. We both knew instinctively that we were family. After reconnecting through Silvio, we began communicating almost every day by email. Grace told me about her dream to reopen her father's primary school in her village, so that the children there would have an alternative to being sent to India.

The Tamang villages are some of the poorest in Nepal and can be quite dangerous. One team of survivors from Apple of God's Eye recently went up to a village near Grace's, and were held hostage by traffickers and other ne'er-do-wells for three days! They had to call their bank and pretend to secure a ransom payment before they were allowed to return home.

When I landed at Kathmandu airport with my crew, Grace was part of our welcoming committee. Her face lit up when she saw me in the arrivals corridor. When I finally got through the crowd and out into the open air, we ran into each others arms and hugged it out for at least five minutes.

The next seven days were some of the best days ever. I spent time with Grace and other endearing young people at Apple of God's Eye. We visited our school-sponsored kids and the jewelry artisans at our other partner agencies, Princess Home and Freedom Matters. I met inspiring people who were putting their lives on the line to save children.

Ranjit and Sarah Kunwar, who run the Princess Home for girls and Cry of the Street for boys, work with children who were once living on the streets. There are scores of feral children in Thamel, Kathmandu's tourist district. These children have been abandoned by their parents, and many have been living on the streets for years. They soon become addicted to glue to numb their pain. The little ones are preyed upon by older street kids, and by adults.

"What is the youngest child you ever pulled out of Thamel?" I asked Ranjit.

"Three, maybe four years old," he said.

We met some of these street boys when we went to Thamel. They were dirty and ragged, starving for attention but trying to seem aloof. Their hair was matted and wild.

One boy of about twelve (my son Luke's age) sat down next to me on the sidewalk, elbow to elbow, knee to knee. He seemed happy to be accepted, to have a few moments of positive adult attention. Then, another boy of about the same age came up and began acting out sexually with the boy next to me, kissing his neck and whispering terms of endearment. 'My lovely,' 'My sweetie'.

At first, the boy at my side seemed irritated, but finally he surrendered to it, and the two little boys kissed and groped each other on the sidewalk. Obviously they were reenacting the sexual abuse that is part of their lives on the streets.

I was deeply disturbed by this incident and later acted out my own distress with a totally inappropriate outburst at a World Heritage Site. I wasn't even able to talk to my friends about the incident with the street kids until days later.

In this work, you can easily start to believe you have seen and heard it all. You think nothing can shock or unbalance you. This experience proved how wrong I was in that assumption. It also increased exponentially my admiration for Ranjit and Sarah.

Helping this population is hard. Many people have tried and given up. The boys are addicted to glue and accustomed to their lives on the streets. In most cases, they run away from shelters and back to the streets when the glue calls to them. As I witnessed, they often act out their pain on others.

I asked Ranjit how he succeeded with these boys where so many others failed. He shared the fact that he himself is a recovering addict. Although he comes from a privileged background in India, he nearly destroyed his life through heroin addiction.

Because of his personal history, Ranjit is able to meet the boys on their own level, without judgment or pity. Just like the in-brothel counselors who forge a relationship of trust with girls in a brothel prior to a rescue raid, Ranjit takes months building relationships with the street kids and gaining their trust before attempting a rescue.

After a friendship has been established, he and his wife bring the kids in small groups to their church about an hour from central Kathmandu. After church, the kids share a meal with Ranjit and Sarah and their three kids, and have some time to relax and play in a safe place, where no one can hurt them. Then they are driven back to their street home in Thamel.

This process is repeated as many times as necessary, until the children are ready to move off the streets and into the Cry of the Street shelter.

"When *they* ask to come, then you know the time is right," Ranjit told us. "As much as you might want to rush it, especially with the younger ones, that never works. They have to be ready".

Ranjit and Sarah had just finished raising a group of twelve boys – the 'tribe of twelve' as they call it – alongside their three biological children. All are now young adults, working or going to college. Two of the boys from the original tribe of twelve are going to be counselors at the new shelter Ranjit and Sarah are constructing, which will house fifty boys.

Twenty girls are growing up at the Princess Home, and ten of these are in our sponsorship program.

Although we've been supporting this project for three years and several staff members have visited, this was the first time I had personally met the Kunwar family and all the kids. I was beyond impressed by everything Ranjit and Sarah have accomplished, and especially inspired by the fact that they did it as a family, with their own three children.

Some people use their kids as an excuse for not getting involved in social causes: '*I've got my hands full with my own kids right now…I'll do it when they grow up*'. That thinking is backwards, in my opinion. Having your own kids can give you even more energy and motivation to help the world's children. Once you jump in, you find even more strength and energy to continue. There is no better legacy you can leave your children than a legacy of service to humanity.

My time in Nepal flew by, and much too soon, it was our last night. I hadn't spent as much time with Grace as we both wanted, because she was studying for final exams and I was charging all over greater Kathmandu visiting projects.

Grace had to start all over in first grade after her second rescue from trafficking. In three years, she has advanced all the way to ninth.

How do you survive being trafficked twice, and still remain an angel? That is a mystery I will never fully understand.

Grace joined us at Silvio and Rose's house on that last night. We were so happy, like two cats with a bowl of cream, just sitting on the couch chatting and looking at pictures on a laptop. Grace had recently visited her home village for the first time since being repatriated to Nepal. She enjoyed a joyful reunion with her brother and grandmother, who wept to see her alive and well after a three year absence.

Grace's village continues to send many of its children off to India. Most are never seen again. The school is barely operational, with teachers who come only occasionally, and no books or exams. Grace is desperate to get back there as a teacher and stop the flow of girls to India once and for all.

She believes, as I do, that education and employment are the only way to turn the tide in a community where trafficking has become a normal and accepted part of life. Grace is my spiritual daughter in this respect, as in so many others.

I was asking Grace what she was reading in English class, when all of a sudden, she threw herself in my arms and began to sob. I held her tight and stroked her hair while she cried, for two straight hours. Of course, I cried too, Britishness notwithstanding.

This experience was beautiful and profound beyond my ability to describe. I realized as I hugged and comforted Grace while she cried, that this was all I ever really wanted, ever since seeing 'The Day My God Died' ten years ago. From the day I saw that film, I yearned to take a little bit of the survivors' burden from them. I longed to love away some of the hurt and betrayal. I was compelled to put the pieces in place for them to fulfill their beautiful dreams and transform the world with their courage.

As a mother, I ached to hold them in my arms and mother them, but in the early days, this wasn't possible or wouldn't have been appropriate. With Grace, I could finally do all these things.

The losses and sorrows of my own life came into perspective. For the first time since Freedom died, the hurt places inside me were healed.

"I've hoped and prayed for another daughter," I whispered. "And now I've found you". Though her tears, Grace beamed her approval.

At the beginning of this journey, I lost Freedom. Then, for eight years, I worked for other women's freedom. And finally, I found Grace.

53   CARE HARDER

So… here we are, sixteen years after my life was changed in a New York movie theater. The work continues. The love continues. It continues to change lives, including my own.

Through many trials, toils and snares, we've succeeded in building a program that works, and I see tremendous progress in the lives of our survivors. In place of my initial haphazard-but-earnest approach, I now know what I'm doing and have a clear vision for the future of our organization, though I'm still open to surprising and miraculous changes of fortune.

Instead of just me, alone in rural Thailand with no contact number and no way to charge my laptop, I am now part of an incredibly talented and dedicated team in the U.S. and in Asia. With their skills and fortitude, anything is possible.

Our teams of artisans are now led by the survivors themselves. We have helped several women to launch their own businesses and expect many more survivor businesses to spin off in the coming years.

John and I have found a way to work together harmoniously, at least 95% of the time. Thanks to my father and stepmother, we have a roof over our heads. Maya and Luke are in college, pursuing their own wild dreams, and have internalized our values around human rights and poverty. They have no weird issues that I can detect. Because of our choice to do this work, John and I haven't been able to give them every advantage that our friends have given their kids, but we have modeled for them the conviction that love can change the world. That is a legacy I am proud to leave my children.

One of the women in our program once told me "You know those people, whose every dream comes true? Well, now I am one of them".

Well, I am one of them too.

Of course, everything is far from perfect. The challenges we face are still enormous. Government responses to trafficking in the areas where we work are inadequate. Many people still ignore the issue or blame the victims. Raising funds to maintain our projects is a continuing challenge.

The survivors struggle through their trauma and their lives are often unstable. Someone is always running away, eloping or getting typhoid, falling apart, or getting repatriated at the worst possible moment.

In a parable from Hindu scripture, King Rama's wife Sita was abducted by a monster, and held captive in Sri Lanka, eighty miles across the ocean from India. The king's army began building a bridge across the ocean to rescue her. All the people and animals joined in the effort, dragging huge boulders and logs to add to the bridge. A tiny squirrel looked down from her tree and wanted to help. She was too small to carry even the smallest stones, so she jumped in the water, rolled in the sand, and then shook off the sand from her body to add to the bridge, over and over again. With her help, the bridge was built and Sita was saved.

The moral of this story (as far as I can tell, since Hindu scripture is nothing if not cryptic) is that you don't need to have amazing resources or skills to make a difference. The squirrel did not have the resumé for stacking boulders. She had no secret stash of stones to contribute to the cause. She only had herself, and her tiny squirrelly self seemed insignificant in the face of the challenge at hand. Despite her limitations, she gave her whole self to the problem. She threw herself into it, literally and figuratively. And that's what it's going to take to change things in this world – people willing to be the squirrel.

We need an army of people prepared to go 'all in', to throw themselves into solving the world's most urgent problems.

"So many people seem to care about global issues, like poverty and lack of clean water and hunger and slavery. I don't see why we aren't making more of an impact on these problems," I complained to my friend Robin. After a long pause, she replied. "Maybe we need to care harder".

There are over one billion people on planet earth living in 'absolute poverty', on less than a $1.25 a day. That's not enough to sustain a person, even in the poorest part of the world. Meanwhile, over half the world's population now belongs to the middle class, 'having a reasonable amount of discretionary income… and roughly a third of their income left after paying for basic food and shelter'.

Imagine if each of us (or even one in every hundred of us) in the middle class took responsibility for one or two people in the less-than-a-dollar-a-day category? What if we each made it our mission to help one person radically improve his or her life? We could reduce absolute poverty to a fraction of what it is today…

For those of you who dare to go all in, it will sometimes be a lonely road. I quoted the Indian poet Tagore at the beginning of this book: *'If you call and no one answers, go anyway'*.

Many people will not want to look at the worst suffering at all. Others will be paralyzed by the enormity of the problems, or repelled by the horror of them. Some will be too busy or distracted to care, or will distance themselves from the problem because they mistakenly think it only happens in other countries, or because they feel they can only afford enough compassion for people in their own town. You can be sure some people will criticize, and since you will (hopefully) be making many mistakes on the way to finding your path, there will surely be plenty of things to criticize. So be it.

Once you start moving forward, people will be inspired by your example and will join you. You will find others already on the path. I have introduced many heroes in this book and there are many more heroes everywhere. You can be a hero, a human bridge between wretchedness and a bright future for a person in need, or ten people, or five thousand.

Like me, you may lose many things you thought you needed and wanted. Things will not go as planned. What you will find is beyond measure:

The wild, unbound joy of children dancing in a courtyard.

The satisfaction, mixed with disbelief, on a young woman's face as she receives her first paycheck.

A slowly growing awareness and compassion in yourself and your family and friends

The pride of seeing a girl — once abused in a brothel with no hope of any kind of future — graduating from high school.

The transformation of a room, a building, a neighborhood, or an entire community.

The flash of hope returning to a person no longer hungry or thirsty, endangered or enslaved.

This is no ordinary joy.

If you enjoyed this book, please review it on Amazon. Thank you!

HOW THIS BOOK CAME TO BE

'This is No Ordinary Joy' would never have been finished without the loving support and help of some dear friends.

My friend Nicole Evans was sitting poolside with me and a couple of margaritas disguised as water bottles, as I bemoaned the fact that I hadn't written a word in six months, since my laptop had been stolen in an airport with a year's worth of writing on it (Please let's not discuss the fact that I should have backed up my computer more often. I get it!) I started telling her the story I had been writing.

"Why don't you just email me one chapter every night?" she suggested. "Write it just the way you're talking to me now, girlfriend to girlfriend. Keep it real. And I'll do my best to edit it for you." Nicole turned out to be an insightful editor and writing coach. By the end of the summer, I had fifty chapters written. I don't know if I ever could have finished this book without her cheerleading ('I loved this chapter, your best yet!') and helpful suggestions ('I think you can leave out the bit about the shredded nipples, it's too much for people').

John Berger, best friend, husband, and right-hand man, made this story possible by throwing his heart, soul and life into the work with me, and encouraging me day in and day out as I wrote our story. Through the years, he's encouraged me to try everything, to not be afraid or ashamed of failure as it is necessary for success, and to face my pain and keep moving forward.

Paul Suit provided herculean proofreading and moral support as I neared the end of the writing process, and his eight years of service in Calcutta helped to give this book its happy ending.

ACKNOWLEDGEMENTS

I would like to thank my family - Maya and Luke Symons Berger, Freedom Ford, Phil and Ann Symons, Calvin and Elizabeth Berger, Brookie Maxwell, Joanne O'Keefe, Judith Ford, Anjali Tamang, Neill Symons, Tamara Massong, Jacqui Ford and Leila Bolitho for their love and support during this joyful and arduous journey.

Huge thanks to my teammates past and present – Heather Deyo, Diane Beale, Jeanette Pavini, Paul Suit, Dianna Badalament, Nancy Edwards, Soma Seal, Nafiza Khatun, Maura Hurley, Sarah Annay Williamson, Aslyn Baringer, Angela Walter, Beth and Tim Tiger, Shira Weinert Cornfeld and family, Helena Geng, Elizabeth Goldberg, Aloka Mitra, Alicia MacGregor, Kimberly Medeiros, Bruce Netherwood, Tia Andrews, Debra Rouse. Theresa Bryne and Bernadette England, Becky Bavinger, Doel Basu, Tiffany Weston, Meg and Kev McCarthy-Schmitz, Sue Ann Heutink, Robin Rossmanith, Susie Carey and Amy Haynie.

I would never have gotten anywhere without our partners past and present – Women's Interlink Foundation, South Kolkata Hamari Muskan, Divine Script, Ektara Community Foundation, Apple of God's Eye, Mirror Foundation, AFESIP, Sanlaap, Ektara, Rescue Foundation, Maiti Nepal, Friends of Maiti Nepal, ChoraChori, Princess Home, Rahab, DEPDC, and Polaris Project

Thanks to all those who believe in this work and have helped make it possible, including Humanity United, Tarsadia Foundation, AIMLoan, Seva Foundation, Naved Khan family, Adrienne and David Keisel, Foster Family Foundation, Hahn Family Foundation, the Schmidt family, Annenberg Foundation and Lush Cosmetics Foundation.

To these dear and heroic people, and all who have believed in me, in our survivors and in their enormous potential, Thank You!

Made in the USA
Middletown, DE
02 March 2020